Adult January Bible Study

ACTS: The Gospel for All People

J. W. MacGorman

CONVENTION PRESS ● NASHVILLE, TENNESSEE

Contents

© Copyright 1990 CONVENTION PRESS
All rights reserved.
5403-91

Dewey Decimal Classification Number: 226.6
Subject Heading: BIBLE N.T. ACTS
Printed in the United States of America.

This book is the text for a course in the subject area Bible Study of the Church Study Course.

Target group: This book is designed for adults and is part of the Church Study Course offerings. The 1963 statement of "The Baptist Faith and Message" is the doctrinal guideline for the writer and editor.

A Word to Begin

Acts is one of the most crucial books in all the New Testament. It forms the bridge between the Gospels and the Epistles. Without the benefit of Acts we would be without most of the history of the early church. Luke's purpose in writing Acts was twofold: (1) To demonstrate the continuing ministry of the risen, ascended Christ, who had been loosed from the restraints of a physical body, and continued working in the Person of the Holy Spirit; (2) to show the progress of the gospel, empowered by the Spirit, as it broke through barriers to carry out Jesus' commission (Acts 1:8). This study of Acts can help you gain a renewed commitment to the exciting new venture that Jesus gave the church. That venture was and is to give bold witness of the gospel to all people.

The textbook may be used in personal or group study. In both uses, the Personal Learning Activities at the end of each chapter will help the learner review the material that has been covered. The *Teaching Guide* will aid the teacher in directing the study. The *Teaching Resource Kit for Acts: The Gospel for All People* contains visuals and other materials that will help the teacher in guiding the study. In this textbook, guidance for using Personal Learning Activities is in the section entitled "The Church Study Course" at the end of the book. The Personal Learning Activities were written by Dr. Jerry W. Lemon, Pastor, Garden Oaks Baptist Church, Houston, Texas.

Also at the back of the book is a Church Study Course Credit request (Form 725). On completing this book, the pupil should mail the complete form to the indicated address.

James D. McLemore, editor

1

The All-inclusive Gospel

Acts 1:1—2:47

Luke was the only Gospel writer who provided an account of Christian beginnings from John the Baptist's birth to Paul's imprisonment in Rome. The other writers—Matthew, Mark, and John—ended their Gospels with the resurrection or ascension of Jesus Christ. In different ways, they bore testimony to God's triumph over sin and death in the first Easter and exaltation of our Lord.

What if Luke had not written the Book of Acts as a sequel to his Gospel? Then we would have a New Testament with four Gospels, twenty-one letters, and John's apocalypse. To be sure, by gleaning historical data and allusions from these writings, we could gain valuable information about the earliest Christian communities. Yet there would be so much that we would not know.

What happened in Jerusalem and beyond in the immediate aftermath of the crucifixion, resurrection, and ascension of Jesus Christ? By overlapping the events described in Luke 24 and Acts 1, along with the repeated dedication to Theophilus (Luke 1:3; Acts 1:1), Luke combined the two works. In both Luke 24:46-48 and Acts 1:8, the risen Lord commissioned his followers to preach the gospel to all nations, Gentiles as well as Jews. This vital theme of world evangelism runs throughout the two-volume work, Luke-Acts. It was present at the beginning in the temple, when devout Simeon took the infant Jesus in his arms and praised God for the salvation He had prepared for all peoples (Luke 2:29-32). Likewise it was prominent in Acts 1:8, where the mission field ranged from Jerusalem to the ends of the earth.

Since God is one, He is the God of all peoples. No nation, race, social class, sex, age category, or denomination of churches can stake out an exclusive claim on God. The gospel of Jesus Christ is for everyone. The gospel is God's redemptive plan for all. The gospel is *all-inclusive!*

How will Jesus Christ's followers accomplish the awesome task of witnessing to a lost world? What power possibly could be equal to the assignment? Once again, both in his Gospel and in Acts, Luke pointed in the same direction. In Luke 24:49 the risen Christ commanded His followers to stay in Jerusalem until they were endued with power from on high. And in Acts 1:8, the same Lord promised and commanded: "You shall receive power when the Holy Spirit has come upon you; and you shall be My witnesses both in Jerusalem, and in all Judea and Samaria, and even to the remotest part of the earth."

Indeed, verse 8 suggests the broad outline of the Book of Acts. For Acts 1:1—8:3 describes witnessing in Jerusalem from the day of Pentecost to the martyrdom of Stephen. Acts 8:4—12:25 describes witnessing in Judea and Samaria primarily. However, Paul's conversion en route to Damascus (9:1-30) and the earliest preaching in Antioch (11:19-30) occurred during this time. And Acts 13:1—28:31 describes witnessing from Antioch of Syria to Rome. Here primary attention falls on Paul and his fellow missionaries. The account ends with Paul under some form of house arrest in Rome. There he spent two years, "welcoming all who came to him, preaching the kingdom of God, and teaching concerning the Lord Jesus Christ with all openness, unhindered" (28:30-31).

The limitations of this book do not permit a commentary on all twenty-eight chapters of Acts. However, our theme is *Acts: The Gospel for All People*, and passages highlighting this theme have been chosen for special emphasis and rewarding study. Nor can concerns regarding text, title, literary setting, authorship, date, and purpose receive their proper due here.

If you read widely, you will encounter differences of opinion regarding all these historical issues. For example, some scholars hold that Luke, "the beloved physician" (Col. 4:14) and Paul's missionary companion, was the author, even though the author of Luke-Acts never gave his name. Others may use the name "Luke" as a convenience, while making it clear that they mean some later, unknown writer. Dates proposed for Acts range from the early sixties, before the outcome of Paul's trial in Rome, to the middle of the second century. For some, the author was a historian of the apostolic age, whereas for others he was a preacher during the final years of the first century. "Whatever his purpose, Luke wrote history; whatever his specific purpose, he intended to inform his readers about the past."[1]

In this study I am assuming that Luke, Paul's physician friend, wrote Acts in the early seventies. His primary purpose was to describe how the gospel overcame many religious, cultural, and geographical barriers as it moved out from Jerusalem to Rome. His secondary purpose was to show that Christianity was the true fulfillment of Jewish hope and offered no subversive threat to Rome.

The Promise of the Father (1:1-14; Focal: 1:1-14)

Luke began his second writing with a prologue that related it to his Gospel. He repeated his dedication to Theophilus (see Luke 1:3). The name Theophilus means "friend of God." He is the only person mentioned in the New Testament to whom writings have been dedicated. His identity and status remain obscure. Luke also reiterated the certainty of the resurrection appearances of Jesus (See Luke 24:13-49). He referred again to the Father's ancient promise—fulfilled at Pentecost—that would launch a new phase in the redemptive story he longed to tell. The Holy Spirit's dramatic outpouring on that epochal occasion would empower Christians for the task of world missions. Indeed, all of Acts 1 sets the stage for the events of the Day of Pentecost, described in chapter 2. And in a real sense, all the remaining chapters of Acts result from Pentecost.

The Prologue (vv. 1-5)
Luke's reference to his Gospel as an account of "all that Jesus began to do and teach" (v. 1) suggested that his second writing would be a continuation of the same story. Both in his Gospel and in Acts, Jesus Christ remained the primary subject.

In the former, Luke testified regarding Jesus' ministry on earth; in the latter, His continued ministry from heaven. Most of the Gospel described what took place before the resurrection; all of Acts portrayed what took place after the resurrection. The Gospel ended and the Book of Acts began in the first Easter.

How will the exalted Lord extend His kingly rule in the hearts of all peoples? Verses 4-5 provide the answer. Having gathered His followers together, he told them to wait for the Father's promise (v. 4) soon to be fulfilled. They were not to leave Jerusalem. Then He described the Father's promise to baptize the apostles with or in the Holy Spirit (v. 5).

At this point we need to probe the meaning of Holy Spirit baptism. This is necessary, because much misunderstanding has arisen regarding this great promise.

The expression "baptized with or in the Holy Spirit" occurs only six times in the entire New Testament. (1 Cor. 12:13 is not considered here.) Four of these occurrences are in the Gospels, where John the Baptist was relating his ministry as forerunner to the ministry of Jesus (Matt. 3:11; Mark 1:8; Luke 3:16; John 1:33). In each instance John spoke of his baptizing with water, whereas the greater Coming One would baptize with the Holy Spirit. Two occurrences are in Acts. One is in Acts 1:5, where Jesus was speaking of John's ministry in relation to His own: "John baptized with water, but you shall be baptized with the Holy Spirit not many days from now." Obviously, Jesus was referring to the imminent outpouring of the Holy Spirit on the day of Pentecost. A second occurrence is in Acts 11:16, where Peter recalled the Lord's teaching about John's baptism with water as preparation for His baptism with the Spirit. Here they are—six references only in the New Testament to this expression—and all in the same basic context. Thus, what was Luke's favorite way of describing the vital Holy Spirit's presence and power in the lives of Christians? The answer is found in the verb "fill" or the adjective "full." Again and again, as we shall see, Acts describes believers as either being "filled with" or "full of" the Holy Spirit. Now note one further truth. In Acts, the greatest evidence of the Holy Spirit's presence and power is bold witnessing to God's redemptive achievement through

Jesus Christ, His Son.

Some churches tend to interpret Holy Spirit baptism as a second work of grace, evidenced by speaking in tongues. They teach that we can be saved without experiencing Holy Spirit baptism. But if we receive "the second blessing," we will know it, because we will speak in tongues as its initial and confirming sign. To me this is a grave error. Not speaking in tongues (glossolalia) but bold witnessing to God's saving grace through Jesus Christ is the primary evidence of the Spirit-filled life in the Book of Acts. The same is true today.

The Commission (vv. 6-11)

In verses 6-11, the disciples inquired about the restoration of the kingdom to Israel (v. 6). Jesus rebuked them for trespassing on divine prerogative (v. 7). He quickly turned their attention back to the imminent out-pouring of the Holy Spirit that would empower them for world witnessing (v. 8). Then He ascended into heaven, from whence at the time of God's choosing He will return in triumph (vv. 9-11).

Restoration of the Kingdom to Israel (vv. 6-8).—Less than a century earlier, in 63 B.C., the Jews had lost their political independence to the Romans. Pompey, a renowned military leader, had conquered Jerusalem, entered the holy of holies in the temple, and had reduced the Jewish state to a Roman province. Thereafter, Rome had governed the Jews through client rulers or Roman procurators, and grieved patriotic Jews. The Jews longed for the coming of a messiah, who would rally the people, run off the Romans, and restore the Jews to national independence and prominence. This form of messianic expectation so gripped the apostles that when Jesus first began to speak of His approaching death in Jerusalem, Peter rebuked Him (Mark 8:31-33). The apostles also hoped to see the kingdom of God fulfilled by the restoration of Israel to national independence. Thus when Jesus spoke about the coming fulfillment of the Father's promise, they asked if the kingdom of God would be restored to Israel at this time (v. 6).

Instead of the answer they sought, they received a rebuke from the Lord: "It is not for you to know times or epochs which the Father has fixed by His own authority. " (v. 7). In fact, during His earthly ministry Jesus had told His followers that He Himself did not know the day or hour of His return (Matt. 24:36; Mark 13:32). How remarkable then that from time to time ever since, people have claimed to know the exact time of the Lord's return! Even more lamentable is the large number of sincere Christians who have given these false prophets a second hearing—or bought their books. No person can know what Jesus said He did not know!

Prediction was not the church's task, proclamation was, and is. Thus Jesus turned aside the prophetic question, and repeated the charge that His followers await empowering from on high. Only baptism with or in the Holy Spirit could prepare them for witnessing to a lost world.

The Ascension (vv. 9-11).—Having appeared to His followers after the resurrection, and having instructed them, Jesus ascended into heaven (vv. 9-10). Enthroned there at the right hand of the Father, soon He would send the Holy Spirit. Finally, at the time determined by and known to the Father only, Jesus Christ will return to the earth in majestic triumph (v. 11).

The Upper Room (vv. 12-14)

Following the Lord's ascension from the Mount of Olives, the disciples returned to Jerusalem. The distance traveled was described as a sabbath day's journey (v. 12), or almost three-quarters of a mile. The term does not mean that the event took place on the sabbath. Some have suggested that the upper room where they were staying was the place where Jesus observed the passover with the apostles before His arrest and trials. This can be little more than a guess. Others have proposed that the meeting place was in the home of Mary, the mother of John Mark. At a later time during Peter's imprisonment by Herod Agrippa I, Christians gathered in Mary's home to pray for his release (Acts 12:12).

Verse 13 provides one of the four lists of the apostles in the New Testament. The others are found in Matthew 10:2-4; Mark 3:16-19; and Luke 6:13-16. Except for variations in order and the deletion of Judas Iscariot, the lists in Luke 6:13-16 and Acts 1:13 are the same. In the upper room, the believers continually devoted themselves to prayer. A great spirit of unity prevailed among them, as it always ought to distinguish the people of God. Among those participating in worship were Mary, the mother of Jesus, and His younger brothers (v. 14). This is the only time that Mary is mentioned in the Book of Acts. Acts 1:15-26 describes the selection of Matthias to take the place of Judas Iscariot among the apostles. The qualification for an apostle is set forth in verses 21-22. He must be one who had associated with the Lord and His apostles from the baptism of John until the ascension. Thus, he, too, would be a witness to the resurrection.

Fulfillment at Pentecost
(2:1-47; Focal: 2:1-24,32-39)

Pentecost marked "the fiftieth day" after the offering of the first fruits of the barley harvest during the Feast of Unleavened Bread (Lev. 23:15-16). Sometimes called the Feast of Weeks, it completed a seven-week harvest season with a festival of solemn joy and thanksgiving to God.

As in Jewish observance, Pentecost celebrated the end of a grain harvest. So in Christian history, Pentecost marked the beginning of a harvest of a different kind. Earlier, Jesus had told His disciples, "Do you not say, 'There are yet four months, and then comes the harvest'? Behold, I say to you, lift up your eyes, and look on the fields, that they are white for harvest." (John 4:35). Before this particular day of Pentecost had passed, a harvest of about three thousand souls had confessed Jesus Christ as Lord and had been baptized. Here we will take note of the phenomena of Pentecost (vv. 1-13), Peter's message (vv. 14-36), and the response of the people (vv. 37-47).

The Phenomena (vv. 1-13)—At Pentecost, astounding happenings attended the Holy Spirit's coming. First, a noise like a fierce, rushing wind filled the place where the believers had gathered (v. 2). Then tongues, as of fire, separated and came to rest on each of them (v. 3). And when they were all filled with the Holy Spirit, they "began to speak with other tongues, as the Spirit was giving them utterance" (v. 4).

Both the mighty wind and the fire were symbols of the presence and power of God's Spirit. Had not John the Baptist proclaimed that whereas he had baptized with water, the Coming One would baptize "with the Holy Spirit and with fire" (Matt. 3:11; Luke 3:16)? But what shall we make of the other external evidence of the Holy Spirit's outpouring at Pentecost, namely, speaking in tongues?

The most obvious explanation of speaking in tongues is found in the verses that immediately follow. Verse 6 states that the festival crowd had come to Jerusalem from many countries. The crowd was bewildered, because each person heard the disciples speaking in his own language. The fact that all those speaking were Galileans made this altogether amazing (v. 7).

Observe in verses 9-11 the far-flung countries of the Jewish Dispersion represented among the pilgrims at Pentecost. They extended from Rome and Libya in the west to Parthia and Elam in the east. And they reached from Cappadocia and Pontus in the north to Egypt and the Sinai Peninsula in the south. Or put another way, they came from lands bordering the Mediterranean Sea in the west to those with shores on the Caspian Sea and Persian Gulf in the east. And they came from Roman provinces on the Black Sea in the north to those on the Red Sea in the south. A few moments with an atlas will enable you to appreciate more the distances that devout Jews traveled to observe the Feast of Weeks in Jerusalem.

In these widely scattered lands of the Jewish Dispersion, many different languages and dialects were spoken. The climactic miracle of Pentecost was that the Holy Spirit enabled the disciples to proclaim God's mighty deeds in the pilgrims' native languages (v. 11). And the extraordinary happening caused many to ask in amazement, "What does this mean?" (v. 12). Others jeered, "They are full of sweet wine" (v. 13).

Christians of equal desire to know the truth of God's Word have reached different conclusions about what really happened at Pentecost. Some have maintained that the miracle was one of *hearing* rather than one of *speaking*. That is, the disciples spoke in their native Aramaic (or possibly, Greek), and the pilgrims from many lands were enabled to hear or understand what they were saying. However, the text does not support this shift of the miracle from the tongues of the disciples to the ears of the pilgrims. Others are troubled by a comparison of the miracle of Pentecost with the spiritual gift of "speaking in tongues" as it is described in 1 Corinthians 14. They argue that in both passages, the phenomenon is speaking in foreign languages—languages one has not learned. But whereas this suits Luke's explanation of the miracle at Pentecost in Acts 2, I do not think it fits Paul's description of the spiritual gift in the Corinthian passage.

May I encourage a simple test at this point? Substitute the words "a foreign language" in every reference to speaking in tongues in 1 Corinthians 14. In most instances the context simply cannot carry this sense. For example, "Therefore let one who speaks in a . . . *foreign language* pray that he may interpret" (1 Cor. 14:13). Otherwise he does not know the meaning of his own utterance! Again, "For if I pray in a . . . *foreign language*, my spirit prays, but my mind is unfruitful" (1 Cor. 14:14). No coordination prevails between the normal thinking process and utterance. This cannot describe one speaking in a foreign language. No! the spiritual gift of speaking in tongues in 1 Corinthians 14 is glossolalia, a form of ecstatic utterance.[2]

Still others seek to reconcile Acts 2 and 1 Corinthians 14 at this point by reversing the above pattern. That is, they insist that speaking in tongues is ecstatic utterance or glossolalia in both passages. Some adherents of this view say that Luke was a creative theologian as well as a historian. Thus, he transformed the ecstatic manifestations at Pentecost into a miracle of languages. In doing so, he dramatized a reversal of the tragic confusion of tongues at Babel (Gen. 11:1-9). Then at Pentecost, people from many nations with their different languages were brought into one fellowship by the Holy Spirit's power.[3]

I am uncomfortable with such "theologizing" of the text of Acts, however cleverly conceived and presented. It has Luke creating something that didn't happen and then narrating it as though it were an actual occurrence. To be sure, none of the above interpretations is free from difficulty, and my own opinion is stated tentatively rather than dogmatically. However, I believe that the miracle of Pentecost was *polyglossa*, speaking in foreign languages. It was not glossolalia or ecstatic utterance, as in 1 Corinthians 14.

Peter's Message (vv. 14-36).—As a consequence of the amazing events of Pentecost, a large crowd gathered, and Peter addressed them (v. 14). First, he refuted the slanderous charge of drunkenness that the mockers had leveled against the disciples. After all, nine o'clock in the morning was hardly the hour associated with intoxication (v. 14)! Then he explained the phenomena of Pentecost as the fulfillment of God's promise through the prophet Joel (vv. 16-21). Having done this, he centered his message in the proclamation of Jesus Christ as God's Anointed One or Messiah (vv. 22-36).

Some knowledge of the Old Testament concept of the Day of the Lord is essential to an understanding of vv. 16-21. The term appears first in Amos 5:18-20, where the prophet boldly challenged the false hope that prevailed among his people. Israel thought that the Day of the Lord would be a time of national vindication. God would intervene in history dramatically to bring judgment on Israel's enemies and to establish His rule in her midst. However, Amos proclaimed that the Day of the Lord would be a time of *divine* vindication rather than *national* victory. This meant that God's judgment would fall on Israel because of her sins, as well as on surrounding sinful peoples. For Israel to long for the coming of the Day of the Lord was to invoke her own judgment. Several other Old Testament passages predict the approaching Day of the Lord; for example, Isaiah 13:6-16; 22:5; Zephaniah 1:14-18; 2:1-3; and Malachi 4:1. Generally the prospect includes God's sudden intervention in the affairs of men, bringing judgment on His enemies and deliverance to the faithful. Cosmic upheaval which shakes the universe to its foundations attends its coming. In the New Testament the Day of the Lord becomes the day of Jesus Christ. In His ministry, God penetrated the present, evil age (Gal. 1:4). Thus believers may enjoy initially all the blessings of God's presence that they are destined to experience fully at the end. The particular blessing of the "last days" described in Peter's quotation of Joel 2:28-32 was the powerful outpouring of the Holy Spirit at Pentecost (vv. 17-18). As a consequence of this fulfillment of the Father's promise (1:4-5), His servants, both men and women, would prophesy. This, Peter affirmed, was the true explanation of what the crowd at Pentecost was seeing.

In 2:22 Peter began to proclaim that Jesus Christ was the promised Messiah. He supported his claim by presenting three lines of evidence. First, the miracles that God performed through Jesus attested to His messiahship (v. 22). Peter assumed that his hearers knew about these mighty works and signs. Second, Jesus' resurrection attested to His messiahship (vv. 23-32). Verse 23 describes the crucifixion both from the vantage-point of God's "predetermined plan and foreknowledge" and human responsibility. No effort was made to reconcile the two concepts or to reduce the inevitable tension between them. The cross was no surprise to God. Yet, this in no way lessened the responsibility of those people who sought

Jesus' crucifixion. The people who crucified Jesus were accountable for what they did and today we too are accountable for our sin.

But the story did not end on a hill outside an ancient city wall. Death did not have the last word. For "God raised Him up again, putting an end to the agony of death, since it was impossible for Him to be held in its power" (v. 24). And ever since, it has been Easter! In the following verses, Peter appealed to his Bible, our Old Testament, to support his claim regarding Jesus' resurrection. Verses 25-28 are from the Septuagint version of Psalm 16:8-11. Peter argued that God's promise to David in this passage had its fulfillment in Jesus' resurrection.

The third evidence of Jesus' messiahship in Peter's message at Pentecost was the outpouring of the Holy Spirit (vv. 33-36). Not only had God raised up Jesus from the dead but He also had exalted Him to a position of power at His right hand. There, having received the promise of the Father, Jesus had poured the Holy Spirit on His followers at Pentecost. Again, Peter appealed to the Scriptures to support his claim. This time he cited Psalm 110:1. He argued that since David had not ascended into heaven, the promise had its fulfillment in Jesus, the Messiah.

Peter closed his message with a bold appeal for decision: "Therefore let all the house of Israel know for certain that God has made Him both Lord and Christ—this Jesus whom you crucified" (v. 36).

The Jewish leaders had decreed that Jesus should die as a blasphemer (Mark 14:61-64). But in the resurrection and exaltation of Jesus, God reversed the verdict. They crucified Him, but God raised Him up. And to this central affirmation of the gospel of Jesus Christ, Peter and his companions bore witness.

The People's Response
(vv. 37-47; Focal: vv. 37-39)

Peter's sermon at Pentecost, empowered by the Holy Spirit, brought conviction to the hearers, and they cried out, "Brethren, what shall we do?" (v. 37) The best response to a direct question is an equally direct answer, and Peter gave it, "Repent, and let each of you be baptized in the name of Jesus Christ for the forgiveness of your sins; and you shall receive the gift of the Holy Spirit" (v. 38). Repentance demanded a radical turning from sin to God. By submitting to baptism the believer made public his confession of faith in Jesus Christ as Lord.

Verse 38 has long been subjected to distortions. On the one hand some people over interpret the emphasis on baptism, making it essential to salvation. This is the view of baptismal regeneration, which teaches that apart from baptism one cannot be saved. In my opinion, this is a legalistic error. On the other hand are those who misinterpret "the gift of the Holy Spirit" as speaking in tongues. Yet nowhere in the record of Pentecost does it say that the three thousand converts spoke in tongues. Nor were the hands of the apostles laid on them. Rather they all received the Holy Spirit, who Himself was the gift bestowed. F. F. Bruce comments: "The gift of the Spirit is the Spirit Himself, bestowed by the exalted Lord under the Father's authority; the gifts of the Spirit are those spiritual faculties which the Spirit imparts, as he 'apportions to each one individually as he wills' (1 Cor. 12:11)."[4]

Acts 2:42-47 describes the afterglow of Pentecost. The new converts devoted themselves to the apostles' teaching, and participated in a fellowship that had its common bond in Jesus Christ (v. 42). Many signs and wonders were accomplished through the apostles (v. 43). A great spirit of unity and generosity prevailed among them (vv. 44-45). They worshiped in the temple; they enjoyed fellowship meals; and they praised God, enjoying favor with the people (vv. 46-47). No wonder then that the Lord was able to add daily to the number of the converts.

Lessons for Life from Acts 1:1—2:47

Today as always, the greatest need in our churches and individual lives is for empowering by the Holy Spirit.—Jesus began His public ministry by submitting to baptism at the hands of John the Baptist. At that time, the Holy Spirit descended on Him, anointing Him with the power to fulfill His messianic mission (Matt. 3:16; Mark 1:10; Luke 3:22). At Pentecost the Holy Spirit came on the church in Jerusalem, to empower it for the task of proclaiming the gospel to a lost world. To attempt the work of God without the power of God is not only a vast presumption but also it guarantees failure.

Jesus' cross and resurrection remain the heart of gospel proclamation.—The apostles' desire to probe the details of the end-time earned the rebuke of the risen Lord (Acts 1:7). This was so, because end-time curiosity ironically thrives at the expense of true global witnessing. Otherwise, Jesus would have encouraged it. One can repudiate the gospel by outright denial or by shifting the center of proclamation from the cross and resurrection to any other Christian belief. The second coming of Jesus Christ will provide no hope for those who have not met Him at the cross and empty tomb.

The primary evidence of the Holy Spirit's presence and power in believers' lives is bold witnessing about Jesus Christ.—Prophetic utterance, rather than ecstatic utterance, is the foremost expression of the Spirit's presence in a congregation. This is true both in the Book of Acts and 1 Corinthians 14. To confuse any one of the spiritual gifts with the Holy Spirit received as a gift in conversion is a sad error.

Not all the sorrow that issues from sin is the godly sorrow that leads to repentance and life.—At Pentecost many hearers were convicted of their sins, and saved through faith in Jesus Christ as Lord. But lots of tears shed over the consequences of sin have nothing to do with repentance toward God. Rather they express nothing more than worldly sorrow that produces death: "For the sorrow that is according to the will of God produces a repentance without regret, leading to salvation; but the sorrow of the world produces death" (2 Cor. 7:10).

---

1. Frank Stagg, *The Book of Acts* (Nashville: Broadman Press, 1955), 17.
2. For further discussion see J. W. MacGorman, "Glossolalic Error and Its Correction: 1 Corinthians 12—14," *Review and Expositor*, LXXX, no. 3 (Summer, 1983), 389-400.
3. William Neil, "The Acts of the Apostles," *New Century Bible* (Greenwood, S.C.: The Attis Press, Inc., 1973), 71-73.
4. F. F. Bruce, *The Book of the Acts* (Grand Rapids, MI: Wm. B. Eerdmans Pub. Co., 1988), 71.

Personal Learning Activities

1. Underline the correct answer. God's redemptive plan is for (1) Jews only, (2) Gentiles only, (3) all persons of every nation.

2. True _____ False _____ Acts 1:8 is a good outline of both the Book of Acts and of how the gospel spread to the world.
3. Underline the correct answer. Traditional scholarship holds that Acts was written by: (1) Luke, a physician; (2) James, the brother of Jesus; (3) Apollos, the Christian orator.
4. True _____ False _____ Acts is a continuation of the story begun in the Gospel according to Luke.
5. Dr. MacGorman states that the primary evidence of being filled with the Holy Spirit in Acts is _____ .
6. True _____ False _____ The disciples expected Jesus to establish His earthly kingdom immediately (1:6-7).
7. In Christian history, Pentecost marked the coming of the _____ _____ and the beginning of a harvest of _____ .
8. Three happenings when the Holy Spirit came at Pentecost were: (1) _____ , (2) _____ , and (3) _____ (2:1-4).
9. True _____ False _____ Dr. MacGorman believes that "tongues" speaks of foreign languages in Acts and ecstatic utterances in 1 Corinthians.
10. Some who heard the believers speaking in tongues accused them of being _____ (2:12-13).
11. List three evidences given by Peter that Jesus is Messiah and Lord (2:22-36) (1) _____ , (2) _____ , (3) _____ .
12. Peter climaxed his sermon by declaring, "Let all the house of _____ know for certain that God has made Him both _____ and _____ this Jesus whom you _____" (2:36).
13. List two things Peter promised if they would "repent," and "be baptized in the name of Jesus Christ" (2:38). (1) _____ (2) _____ .
14. Some characteristics of the early church were (2:41-47):

_____

_____

_____ .

Answers: 1. (3). 2. True. 3. (1). 4. True. 5. Bold witnessing to God's redemption in Christ. 6. True. 7. Holy Spirit, souls. 8. Noise like a great wind, tongues of fire, speaking with other tongues. 9. True. 10. Drunk. 11. Miracles, Jesus' resurrection, the outpouring of the Holy Spirit. 12. Israel, Lord, Christ, crucified. 13. Forgiveness of sins and the gift of the Holy Spirit. 14. Baptism, teaching, fellowship, breaking of bread, prayers, unity, sincerity, acceptance by people.

18

2

Sharing the Good News Boldly

Acts 3:1—5:42

The only world we know is one that found Jesus Christ, the matchless Son of God, intolerable. It nailed Him to a cross. Had He lived in the world at any prior or subsequent time, the outcome likely would have been the same. Only the form of execution might have been different. This is true because of who He is and because of what sin does.

In His earthly ministry, Jesus proclaimed the good news of the kingdom of God, calling on people everywhere to repent and believe the gospel (Mark 1:14-15). He healed the sick, He fed the hungry, He gave hope to outcasts, and He blessed children. Yes, but He also refused to be bound by the religious traditions that choked God's law while trying to preserve it. He drove from the temple those whose greed had turned the place of prayer into a den of thieves. Eventually, the people chose Him to die instead of Barabbas, a murderer. Then Pilate ordered His crucifixion.

No stranger to hostility, Jesus tried to prepare His followers for persecution. In the Beatitudes, He pronounced blessed those who endured persecution for righteousness' sake (Matt. 5:10-12). Also, Jesus warned that His followers would be delivered up to councils, be beaten in synagogues, and be brought before governors and kings for His sake (Matt. 24:9; Mark 13:9; Luke 21:12). In such circumstances, they were not to fret over what they should say. The Holy Spirit would supply the needed wisdom and words (Matt. 10:19-20; Mark 13:11; Luke 21:14-15).

The Book of Acts provides many instances of the Spirit's support during persecution. Indeed, shortly after Pentecost, the healing of a lame beggar triggered a whole chain of events that found the apostles in and out of prison.

The Healing of a Lame Beggar
(3:1-10; Focal 3:1-8)

At the ninth hour, or about three o'clock in the afternoon, Peter and John went up to the temple to pray. This was the time of the evening sacrifice, and a service of public prayer accompanied it. Following Pentecost the earliest Christians still worshiped God in the temple services. As they approached the temple, they met a beggar sitting at the gate called Beautiful. None of the nine gates leading into the temple is named "Beautiful" in Jewish sources. Scholars tend to identify it with the one designated elsewhere as the Nicanor Gate.

Many think that this was the gate that led from the Court of the Gentiles into the Court of the Women. This was the usual place for the men to gather for worship during the daily morning and evening sacrifices (Ex. 29:38-39). Balconies in this area accommodated the women, who were not permitted to go any further into the temple.

Acts 4:22 tells us that the man had been lame from birth, and was now over forty years old. Unable to work, he was carried daily to his place at the temple gate, where he begged alms of those entering to worship. He evidently thought that those who turned aside from busy pursuits to pray would be more inclined to have compassion for his disability. As Peter and John drew near, the lame man began to beg, first with his eyes and then with his voice. The response was extraordinary. Instead of a coin, he received a command, as Peter said, "I do not possess silver and gold, but what I do have I give to you: In the name of Jesus Christ the Nazarene—walk!" (v. 6). Then taking him by the right hand, he raised him up, and immediately the man stood up and began to walk. Only someone who had experienced despair for over forty years could understand the unrestrained joy and release of the healed man. Not content to walk freely for the first time in his life, he began to leap and to praise God (v. 8). And as the apostles continued on their way into the temple to pray, he joined them. Of course, the leaps of joy and shouts of praise drew the people's attention, and, in amazement, a crowd gathered. The crippled beggar had long been a familiar sight at the temple gate. Now he who always had been carried from place to place was entering the temple with a forceful stride, punctuated with jumps. The whole scene seemed like the fulfillment of an ancient prophecy, "Then the lame will leap like a deer" (Isa. 35:6).

In His earthly ministry, Jesus had healed the diseases of many and enabled the lame to walk. For example, in Capernaum, He had commanded the paralytic borne by four friends to rise, take up his pallet, and go home (Mark 2:11). Then from a throne in heaven, He was continuing His mighty works through the disciples, on whom He had poured out the Holy Spirit at Pentecost.

Peter's Message (3:11-26; Focal: 3:11-21)

For the second time, Peter had the opportunity to proclaim the gospel of Jesus Christ to a large crowd in Jerusalem. As the people, attracted by the miracle of healing, gathered with intense excitement in the portico of Solomon, Peter began to address them.

A Humble Disclaimer (v. 12)

The first thing that Peter did was to disclaim all credit for healing the crippled beggar. He could not bear to have the people attribute the miracle to himself. Had he intoned, "In the name of Peter, the rock, walk," the beggar still would have been begging at the temple gate. The explanation of the miracle did not reside in one of the Lord's servants, but rather in the servant's Lord.

Peter's disclaimer was neither a needless modesty nor a wasted effort, for people are prone to attribute to men what only the Lord can do. In the work of the kingdom of God, "Lord" and "servant" are two categories that never should be confused. If the two roles are confused, immature believers will give to a mere servant like Peter a devotion that rightly belongs only to Jesus Christ as Lord.

When carnal believers in Corinth divided and rallied under the name of celebrity servants (1 Cor. 1:12), Paul countered,

"What then is Apollos? And what is Paul? Servants through whom you believed, even as the Lord gave opportunity to each one" (1 Cor. 3:5). When sheep mistake the head ram for the shepherd, the flock is doomed to take a nasty tumble over the nearest cliff!

Even more contemptible were those servants in Corinth who encouraged this sad delusion by making lordlike noises. Today, this can be done through media claims of extraordinary audiences with the Lord in which divine power is subcontracted to the celebrity servant. While lesser servants may need to agonize in prayer, the super-servant seems to have a direct hookup with God that authorizes all his pronouncements. These include his political choices as well as his gospel proclamations, and the faithful never are supposed to question the communication. After all, who wants to be found voting against God!

Perhaps the least feared form of robbery is theft of God's glory, and this larceny is one of the occupational hazards of ministry. Fortunately, Peter denied the crowd in Solomon's portico the delusion of attributing the miracle of healing to his own power or piety.

A Repeated Charge (vv. 13-16)

At Pentecost, Peter had charged his Jewish hearers with nailing Jesus Christ to the cross through the hands of godless men (2:23). Now he repeated the dreadful accusation, adding the details about Pilate's intention to release Him and the people's choice of Barabbas (vv. 13-14). At no point was their shame in sharper focus than when they disowned "the Holy and Righteous One" and demanded the release of a notorious criminal. In doing so, they had set free a murderer and put to death "the Prince of life" (v. 15).

However, God had reversed the cruel and wicked verdict of the highest court in Israel, the Sanhedrin. He had raised Jesus from the dead and exalted Him to a throne at His right hand. Israel's God had overruled Israel's verdict. The "servant" whom Jewish religious leaders had vilified, the God of Abraham, Isaac, and Jacob had glorified. Herein lay the true explanation of the miracle. From His throne in heaven the glorified Christ had made the crippled man whole. Peter had invoked His power when he had commanded the beggar, "In the name of Jesus Christ the Nazarene—walk!" (v. 6). The lame man had responded in faith, and the Lord had given him perfect health in the presence of all (v. 16).

Observe that in biblical thought a man's name was more than just the means of distinguishing him from other men. His name revealed his character; it denoted his essential being or personality. This is why the choosing of a child's name was so important. The same principle was true with our Lord. In Joseph's dream regarding Mary's conception, the angel said, "And she will bear a Son; and you shall call His name Jesus, for it is He who will save His people from their sins" (Matt. 1:21). **Jesus** is the Greek form of the Hebrew name "Joshua," meaning *Deliverer* or *Savior*. This name surely reveals the character and denotes the essential being of the Lord.[1]

A Softened Appeal (vv. 17-26)

Peter softened the severity of the charge against his hearers and their leaders by allowing that they all had acted in ignorance. They did not recognize Jesus of Nazareth as the Messiah for whom they had waited so long. Thus Peter's explanation was in keeping with the spirit of Jesus' prayer on the cross for His enemies, "Father, forgive them; for they do not know what they are doing" (Luke 23:34).

Popular messianic hope had looked for a great leader who would rally the people and run the Romans out of the land. He would restore the kingdom to Israel and lead it to greater heights and glory than it had enjoyed under David. Even John the Baptist, the divinely appointed forerunner of Jesus, had expected a messiah who would bring summary judgment on the people. The samples of his messianic preaching recorded in the New Testament were weighted heavily with judgment. He warned the Pharisees and Sadducees who came to him for baptism of "the wrath to come" (Matt. 3:7; Luke 3:7). He spoke about the axe that already was chopping down fruitless trees for the fire (Luke 3:9). He spoke of the winnowing fork with which the Messiah would clear His threshing floor, storing the wheat but burning the chaff with unquenchable fire (Luke 3:17).

No wonder that later, John the Baptist was to question Jesus' identity as the Messiah. For when reports of Jesus' deeds reached him in prison, John sent his disciples to ask Jesus, "Are You the Expected One, or shall we look for someone else?" (Matt. 11:3). In response to John's question, Jesus described a ministry in which the blind received sight, the lame walked, lepers were cleansed, the deaf heard, the dead were raised, and the poor were evangelized (Matt. 11:5). These were messianic works, too (see Luke 4:16-21).

Yes, Jesus was the Messiah who fulfilled Old Testament hope, but He was not the kind of Messiah the people expected. Yet through the prophets' teachings, God had made plain that His Christ would fulfill His ministry through suffering (3:18). As the Suffering Servant of God, He would achieve His mission by walking paths of lowliness, humiliation, and eventually death (Isa. 52:13—53:12). The messianic pattern was to be through sufferings to glory (1 Pet. 1:11).

Having offered this explanation, Peter strongly appealed to the crowd assembled in Solomon's colonnade to repent of their sins (Acts 3:19). Then times of refreshing would come from the presence of the Lord, who already was enthroned in heaven "until the period of restoration of all things" (3:21). Jesus was the prophet like Moses, whose coming Moses had prophesied (3:22-23; Deut. 18:15). Moreover, Samuel and all the later prophets had announced these days, when God's promise to Abraham of universal blessing would be fulfilled (3:24-25; Gen. 12:3; 22:18). For God had raised up Jesus, His Servant, and had sent Him first to Israel, to bless them by turning them from their wicked ways (v. 26).

Now was the time for Peter's hearers to repent of their sin of putting to death the Prince of life. Then they would experience the times of refreshment that had been promised. Also, they would be prepared to participate in the grand climax of Jesus' triumphant return to the earth. This, indeed, will be a restoration that includes the world of nature, now in bondage to decay, as well as all the redeemed (Rom. 8:19-22).

Looking back over Peter's sermon to the crowd gathered in Solomon's portico, observe the rich variety of names or titles applied to Jesus. He was called "Servant" (3:13,26), for He fulfilled His messianic mission as the Suffering Servant of God (Isa. 42:1-9; 49:1-6; 50:4-9; 52:13—53:12). He was called "the Holy and Righteous One" (3:14), for He was set apart for God's service and was blameless in character (Acts 7:52; 22:14). He was called "the Prince of life" (3:15), or perhaps better here "the Author of life," as rendered in the Revised Standard Version.[2] By His resurrection from the dead, He has become "the Author of life" or salvation. And He was identified as the "Prophet" like Moses (v. 22), for He was the new lawgiver of the messianic age. To Him all the people must give heed or face dire consequences (vv. 22-23).

Jailed for Preaching the Gospel (4:1-37; Focal: 4:4-13,18-20,29-30,36-37)

All the commotion in Solomon's portico drew the religious authorities' and temple guards' attention. Then they moved nearer to the scene to listen. They became deeply agitated as they heard the disciples "proclaiming in Jesus the resurrection from the dead" (v. 2). Hastily they arrested Peter and John, and put them in jail until they could be brought before the Sanhedrin the next day. However, many who had heard Peter's Spirit-empowered preaching believed, so that the number of men who believed increased to about five thousand (v. 4).

Arraigned before the Sanhedrin (vv. 5-12)

On the following day the Jewish leaders brought Peter and John before the Sanhedrin for trial. At this time, Caiaphas was actually the high priest and president of the Sanhedrin. Annas, however, a former high priest, remained the power behind the office. Five of his sons, one grandson, and Caiaphas, his son-in-law, all served as high priests at various times. Evidently the term "high priest" could have a broader application to members of the families from which the high priests were chosen.[3]

The Sanhedrin asked the disciples directly, "By what power, or in what name, have you done this?" (v. 7). Once again importance was attached to a name. **In what name** means *by whose authority* was this act of healing done? Thus Peter and John found themselves in the kind of harassing circumstances that Jesus had predicted (Luke 21:14-15). And, as He had promised, the Holy Spirit filled them and prompted their response before the Sanhedrin (v. 8).

Earlier Peter had made certain that the crowd gathered in Solomon's portico did not attribute the healing miracle to him. Then before the Jewish council, he likewise disclaimed all credit for the mighty work of healing that had taken place. He declared boldly that it was through "the name of Jesus Christ the Nazarene" that the crippled man had received the power to walk (v. 10). While doing so, Peter underscored again the contrary verdicts of his hearers and God regarding Jesus Christ. They had crucified Him, but God had raised Him up. Further-

more, Peter identified the exalted Lord with the fulfillment of
the stone prophecy of Psalm 118:22,

The stone which the builders rejected
Has become the chief corner *stone.*

In its original setting, the rejected stone likely was Israel.
Other nations had scorned her, but God had chosen her for His
redemptive purpose. However, in the New Testament understanding of the passage, the builders were the Jewish leaders
who rejected Jesus as the Messiah. In fact, in the Parable of the
Vineyard (Luke 20:17) Jesus had so interpreted Psalm 118:22.
But God had overruled their rejection by making Him the chief
cornerstone. He did this by raising Jesus from the dead and exalting Him to the throne of universal power at His right hand.

Return for a moment to the scene in the Gospels where Peter
denied the Lord, after having pledged loyalty even to death
(Matt. 26:35,69-75; Mark 14:29,66-72; Luke 22:33,54-62). While
the Sanhedrin was questioning Jesus, Peter waited outside in
the courtyard. A girl saw him and charged, "This man was with
Him too" (Luke 22:56). Peter denied that he even knew Jesus.
Others thought they recognized him as a follower of Jesus, but
twice more Peter vigorously denied the associations. And before the echo of his third denial could be absorbed by the chilly
night air, a rooster crowed, as Jesus had predicted (Luke 22:34).

What had happened to Peter during the brief interval between his denial of Jesus in the courtyard and his bold witness
to him in the court? Now he faced the same Sanhedrin that had
condemned Jesus to die on the cross, and only a few weeks had
elapsed. Yet he was boldly witnessing to Jesus' resurrection
and exaltation in the highest Jewish court. Moreover, without
the benefit of rabbinical schooling, he dared to insist that what
had happened to Jesus fulfilled the Scriptures. The answer, of
course, was that he and the other disciples had been with the
risen Lord. Also, as Jesus had promised, they had been empowered with the Holy Spirit at Pentecost. Now that same Holy
Spirit had granted him boldness to speak before the Sanhedrin.

Peter, the denier, had become Peter, the declarer; Peter, the
reed, had become Peter, the rock!

Even the professional scholars of the supreme Jewish council
marveled at Peter's and John's boldness and declarations.

None of them could remember sitting next to the two in the rabbinical schools. Yet here they were, instructing the Sanhedrin!

Forbidden to Preach the Gospel (vv. 13-22)

When the council deliberated privately, the members faced a dilemma. The presence of the healed beggar made it impossible for them to deny that a miracle had taken place. Yet, they wanted to keep the movement from spreading further among the people. Thus, they determined to command Peter and John "not to speak or teach at all in the name of Jesus" (v. 18).

The council's order, in turn, confronted Peter and John with a dilemma. On the one hand, the risen Lord had commanded them to preach the gospel to the entire world (Acts 1:8). On the other, the Sanhedrin, representing the highest legally vested Jewish authority, had ordered them to preach no more. The Lord's command was thus contradicted by the council's decree.

What should Peter and John do? To be sure, during His earthly ministry, Jesus had taught them to "render to Caesar the things that are Caesar's, and to God the things that are God's" (Luke 20:25). But that instruction dealt with paying taxes. What Peter and John faced was quite different. Legally vested authority (a parallel of Caesar) was demanding that what the Lord had commanded should be done no more. Caesar was demanding the things that belonged to God. The issue was civil obedience at the expense of obedience to the Lord.

The prisoners responded to the council, "Whether it is right in the sight of God to give heed to you rather than to God, you be the judge; for we cannot stop speaking what we have seen and heard" (vv. 19-20). Confronted with the choice between obedience to God or man, Peter and John openly declared their prior allegiance to God. They would disobey, and then take the consequences of their disobedience.

Observe what Peter and John *did not* do. They did not organize a militant, underground movement to assassinate key members of the Sanhedrin. Had they chosen to manifest their zeal for God and His truth in this way, they could have drawn on a long tradition in their history. Remember Simeon and Levi, the sons of Jacob, who murdered the men of Shechem in vengeance for the rape of Dinah, their sister (Gen. 34:1-31). Remember Phinehas, the priest, who ran a spear through the bodies of both an Israelite and his Midianite wife (Num. 25:1-8). Indeed, later Paul would testify that his own zeal for the ancestral traditions led him to persecute the church of God and seek to destroy it (Gal. 1:13-14).

All the zealots were certain that they were serving God by murdering those whom they regarded as enemies of the true faith of Israel. Their descendants sometimes have sought to accomplish with words what their devoted forbears did with knives. Yes, but with the kiss of Judas still wet on His cheek at Gethsemane, Jesus rebuked the disciple who drew a sword to defend Him. He reminded him that if sword power could further God's redemptive purpose, He could mobilize immediately more than twelve legions of angels (Matt. 26:53). Since a legion numbers six thousand, this would represent an angelic army of over seventy-two thousand. Surely the combined might of such a force could have achieved a more impressive carnage than one paltry ear!

Jesus never sought to advance the kingdom of God by wielding a sword. He died for sinners; He did not murder them. Militant Christianity must be a Christianity willing to die, not ready to kill.

To Peter's bold declaration that he placed obedience to God above obedience to men, the Sanhedrin responded with repeated threats (v. 21). However, they had no legitimate grounds to detain them further, so they let the disciples go (v. 21).

Thriving Though Threatened (vv. 23-37)

Following their release, the apostles returned to their fellow-believers, where they reported all that had happened (v. 23). Soon they were united in prayer, and what a prayer it was! In it they praised God, quoted Scripture, and recounted the events that had led up to Jesus' crucifixion (vv. 24-28). Then they asked God to grant them power to proclaim His word with great confidence (v. 29). And they fully expected that He would continue to accomplish mighty works through the name of Jesus, His holy Servant (v. 30).

When persecution threatened, the early Christians in Jerusalem asked the Lord to grant them greater boldness to preach the gospel. They did not whine in God's presence regarding the indignities they had suffered; they did not wallow in despair. Their faith was inclined to neither whimper nor complain. Rather it was triumphant and hopeful.

To be sure, the early Christian community in Jerusalem did not have so much of what we think is necessary to have a thriving church. They had no church building, so a desirable location was not an issue. They lacked rabbinically trained leaders. Though a great spirit of generosity prevailed among them, they likely had a limited budget! Of course, Barnabas set a noble example by selling a tract of land and handing over the money to the apostles (vv. 36-37). Yet their witness for Jesus Christ was reaching thousands in the city. All Jerusalem knew that they were there serving the Lord and ministering to people. God was able to add daily to their number those who were being saved. Great joy, holy excitement, and warm fellowship prevailed among them. They did not *have* a church; they *were* one!

Arrested Again and Beaten
(5:17-32; Focal: 5:25-32,41-42)

Ananias and Sapphira's tragic failure (vv. 1-11) intervenes in the accounts of Barnabas' generosity (4:36-37) and renewed persecution by the Jewish authorities.

By now, as reports of the new movement spread, people from the cities near Jerusalem began to bring their sick to the apostles. Many were healed, and this increased activity and excitement did not escape the Jewish leaders' notice (5:12-16). Once again, they had the apostles arrested and placed in prison for daring to continue their ministries in Jesus' name and to defy the Sanhedrin's order (v. 18). However, this time a miraculous deliverance from prison was attended by the angelic command, "Go your way, stand and speak to the people in the temple the whole message of this Life" (v. 20).

When the council gathered the next day, they sent for the apostles, only to be told that they were not in the prison. This was all the more amazing since those sent reported that the prison doors were locked securely with guards standing duty nearby (v. 23). All were perplexed until someone came to report that the imprisoned apostles were at that moment in the temple teaching the people (v. 25). Whereupon officers were sent to arrest them again and to bring them before the council. There the high priest charged, "We gave you strict orders not to continue teaching in this name, and behold, you have filled Jerusalem with your teaching, and intend to bring this man's blood upon us" (v. 28). But Peter and the other apostles replied, "We must obey God rather than men" (v. 29).

Once again the apostles indicted the Jewish leaders for having Jesus put to death on the cross. Also, they cited Jesus' resurrection and exaltation as God's complete reversal of the Sanhedrin's judgment. Israel needed to repent and to find forgiveness through the one they deemed unfit to live. All their charges and disclosures were undergirded by the witness of the apostles and also the Holy Spirit (v. 32). The apostles' boldness in defying the council's order infuriated the Jewish leaders. Apart from the restraining counsel of Gamaliel, an esteemed teacher of the law, the angry leaders might have slain the apostles (vv. 33-39). Instead the council summoned them back to the court, flogged them, and repeated its warning not to speak any more in the name of Jesus. Then it released the apostles.

Rejoicing in Suffering (5:41-42)

The apostles' response was remarkable. Subjected to the harassment of repeated arrests and humiliated by a court-ordered flogging, they left the council "rejoicing that they had been considered worthy to suffer shame for His name" (v. 41). Again they did not pay an ounce more heed to the council's restricting order. Instead day after day, in the temple and door-to-door, they continued teaching and preaching that Jesus was the Christ (v. 42).

Lessons for Life from Acts 3:1—5:42

The early church in Jerusalem was short on gold and silver, but long on spiritual power.—Needless to say, this proportion can be tragically reversed.

Obedience to God always takes precedence over obedience to men.—Government is essential to order in society, preventing anarchy and making community life possible. Several New Testament passages affirm the Christian's responsibility to be good citizens (Rom 13:1-7; 1 Tim. 2:1-2; 1 Pet. 2:13-17).

We are fortunate to live in a country whose history, constitution, and laws are sensitive to the need for religious liberty. The separation of church and state is an important concept in this heritage. But what is the Christian's responsibility when the state infringes on religious liberty; when legally vested authority demands what one's conscience cannot allow? The answer must be, "We must obey God rather than men" (5:29).

We do not advance the kingdom of God by adopting values and methods that Jesus repudiated in His earthly ministry.— Church history has been marred by chapters in which the dominant group has perpetrated wrong with the rationale: "The end justifies the means." Such logic often has been used to excuse the atrocities of religious persecution. In Christian discipleship the end does not justify the means; it *determines* them. Nothing that is alien to the gospel can advance the cause of Christ. One cannot lie in defense of the truth and one cannot murder dissidents to the glory of God.

The distinction between "Lord" and "Servant" always must be kept in mind.—As a faithful servant, Peter refused to allow people to give him credit for a healing that the exalted Lord had accomplished. All our potential resides in the context of servanthood; none of us is a fit candidate for lordship. This is why it ill behooves any of Christ's servants to make lordlike noises. Indeed, many church and denominational troubles become inevitable when people give mere servants an adoration and loyalty that rightly belongs only to Jesus Christ as Lord.

---

1. "Name," *The Interpreter's Dictionary of the Bible*, Vol. 3 (Nashville: Abingdon Press, 1962), 500-508.
2. *From the Revised Standard Version of the Bible*, copyrighted 1946, 1952, 1971, 1973. Used by permission.
3. See F. F. Bruce, *The Book of Acts*, (Grand Rapids, MI: Eerdmans Pub. Co., 1954), 77-78.

Personal Learning Activities

1. What miracle by Peter and John in the name of Jesus brought glory to God and aroused strong persecution from the high priests (3:1-10)? _____

2. Peter claimed that the man was healed in the ____ ____ ____ (3:16).
3. Peter used the occasion of the healing of the lame man as an opportunity to proclaim the ____ and to call upon the people to ____ and ____ (3:11-16,19).
4. List four titles Peter applied to Jesus in Acts 3:13-26:
   (1) _____ (2) _____
   (3) _____ (4) _____ .
5. True ____ False ____ The persecution and trouble Jesus and His followers faced came as a great surprise (3:18).
6. Luke indicated that the Jews recognized that the confidence of Peter and John was because they had ____ ____ ____ (4:13).
7. True ____ False ____ The majority of the Jewish council accepted Jesus as Savior and did all they could to win others to Him (4:1-12).
8. What did Peter and John say when the Sanhedrin threatened them and told them not to speak in the name of Jesus (4:18-19)? _____ .
9. The source of power for effective ministry and witness by Christians is the _____ _____ (4:31; 1:8).
10. In contrast to Barnabas's ____ (4:36-37), Ananias and Sapphira died for ____ to God (5:1-11)
11. Peter and other apostles responded to further threats by replying: "We must obey ____ rather than ____" (5:29). Then they "kept right on ____ and ____ Jesus as the ____" (5:42).
12. True ____ False ____ A major truth from Acts 5:17-42 is that obedience to God always takes precedence over obedience to men.
13. Consider the four **Lessons for Life** and write down the one that applies most to you at this time. _____ .

3

Faithful Witnesses Overcoming Barriers

Acts 6:1—8:40

The command to preach the gospel to all the world involves overcoming many formidable barriers. Among them none is more serious than dissension in the church. Actually, a divided church has little to offer to a fractured world. The world already has written the manual on how *not* to live together in peace. Furthermore, a climate of contention among believers gives the lie to the gospel that supposedly reconciles alienated people to God and to each other. Dissension reduces the mighty flow of the Holy Spirit to a painful trickle, as evidenced in loveless confrontations, powerless churches, decreasing baptisms, and fewer churches planted.

When the persecution of Christians is linked to specific incidents, and its punishments are limited to judicial floggings and decrees, that is not as difficult to overcome as general persecution. Certainly intensified general persecution constituted an imposing barrier to preaching the gospel.

The differences that prevail between people often pose problems, too. Sometimes these differences move along ethnic or national lines, with their varying cultural patterns and long histories of abuse and prejudice. Such was the case in the long-standing tensions between the Jews and Samaritans. At other times, these differences were factors in the efforts of individuals to relate to each other. One may have come from a distant land, while the other was homegrown, a native whose speech betrayed no foreign accent. One may have occupied a high place in government, while the other enjoyed no conspicuous station in life. One may have had the means for distant travel with a finely crafted chariot drawn by well-bred horses, while the other moved about on well-worn sandals. Such was the case with Philip and the Ethiopian eunuch.

Interestingly, the focal passages chosen for chapter 3 center on overcoming each of these barriers: (1) internal dissension (6:1-7); (2) intensified persecution (7:55—8:8); and (3) individual differences (8:26-40).

Internal Dissension (6:1-7; Focal: 6:1-7)

The careful reader probably will sense a lapse of time between the events described in Acts 1:1—5:42 and the beginning of Acts 6. This was suggested by the general introductory formula that Luke used in continuing his account, "Now in these days" (6:1, RSV).[1] Also, in chapters 1—5 Luke described the early preaching of the gospel to the Jews. Then the gospel spread to the Greek-speaking communities, and a distinction was made between Hellenists and Hebrews. The "Hellenists" usually were identified as Jews, whose native language was Greek, as opposed to the "Hebrews," who spoke Aramaic.

Protest of the Hellenistic Jews (v. 1)

When the Jewish authorities threatened and persecuted the early Christians (Acts 4:1—5:42), the church thrived. A great spirit of joy, excitement, and generosity marked their faith. With courage and power they bore witness to God's saving grace in Jesus Christ. As they witnessed their numbers increased dramatically.

Unfortunately a different spirit had taken over as chapter 6 unfolded. The body of Christ in Jerusalem was described as having the Hellenistic Jews on one side, and native Hebrews on the other. Such distinctions or labels usually mean that believers have lost sight of their common bond in Christ, as lesser considerations become more important.

The ugly charge of discrimination was leveled against the Hebrews by the offended Hellenistic Jews. They complained that their widows were receiving less than the Hebrew widows from the common supply of goods. Thus rejoicing gave way to resentment and love gave way to envy. Proclamation of the gospel was done against the background of grumbling and complaint in the church.

The problem of prejudice is an old one in human history, and it never fails to set in motion a whole wave of destructive forces. Deeply ingrained in our carnal natures is the craving for preferential treatment. Enough is not enough until it is more than others have. Few want equality, no matter how much lip service they pay to the noble ideal. What they want is advantage. Those who want and get it tend to gloat; those who want and don't get it tend to glower. And in history's reversals the gloaters and glowerers often have changed places.

Yet discrimination in all its forms is never as out of place as in the body of Christ. James 2:1 is particularly forceful in Phillips' translation, "Don't ever attempt, my brothers, to combine snobbery with faith in our glorious Lord Jesus Christ!"[2]

Solving the Problem (vv. 2-6)

Faced with ill will and division in the church, the apostles made some definite moves to resolve the problem. First, they spelled out a division of labors, "It is not desirable for us to neglect the word of God in order to serve tables" (v. 2). Here the ministries of "the word of God" and "serving tables" were recognized. By calling and gifting, the apostles were to proclaim the Word of God, undergirded with much time spent in prayer. For them to devote their energies to the administrative tasks of apportioning supplies to the individual needs of widows in the church would have been a diversion. The proclamation of the gospel would have been neglected. God had others in the congregation, whom He could call and equip for the important tasks of administrations. In the enumeration of charismatic offices or functions found in 1 Corinthians 12:28 "administrations" is listed. God called and equipped some for the ministry of proclamation. He called and equipped others for administrative functions in the work of His kingdom, and He gifted some people in both areas of service.

Consequently, the next step found the apostles instructing the church to select from their number seven men to be placed in charge of ministering to the poor (v. 3). Three qualifications were stressed. First, those chosen were to be men of good reputation. Personal integrity was an utter necessity. Second, they

36

were to be men who were full of the Spirit. This emphasis on the fullness of the Holy Spirit in the lives of all believers is consistent with Luke's witness throughout the Book of Acts. And third, they were to be men of wisdom. Certainly those assigned the tasks of receiving provisions, storing them, and then assessing the relative needs of those seeking help needed to have unusual insight.

The responsibility for making the selections belonged to the church. The men who were chosen were not designated by apostolic appointment. The authority resided in the congregation, which, in turn, abided under God's authority.

Also, the seven men chosen had Greek names. They were Stephen, Philip, Prochorus, Nicanor, Timon, Parmenas, and Nicolas. They were not Reuben, Benjamin, Saul, Jacob, and Mordecai! This did not mean that none of the seven was a Palestinian Jew, but it did suggest that the seven were not a stacked committee!

After selections had been made, the church brought the seven before the apostles, who prayed for them and laid their hands on them (v. 6).

The most natural reading of the text suggests that the apostles were the ones who laid hands on them. This sense prevails in the *New International Version* of the New Testament, "They presented these men to the apostles, who prayed and laid their hands on them."[3]

However, some scholars have argued that the entire congregation joined the apostles in laying hands on the seven. Thus Frank Stagg stated, "If the grammatical antecedent is strictly observed, it follows that 'the whole multitude,' not merely the apostles, 'laid their hands upon them' (6:5-6)."[4] Neither rendering could be ruled in or out on technical grounds. Some translations have retained the ambiguity of the original text. More important than the identity of those who laid hands on the seven was the significance of the act.

When we turn to the Old Testament, we find the laying on of hands in various contexts and with different meanings. For example, on the Day of Atonement the high priest laid his hands on the head of the scapegoat, which bore the sins of the people into the wilderness (Lev. 16:20-22). Here the rite signified the transference of guilt from the offerer to the victim. Again, the laying on of hands could signify the bestowal of a blessing, as when Jacob gave his cross-handed blessings to the sons of Joseph (Gen. 48:14). Also, the laying on of hands could signify a commissioning to a role of leadership. This was true in Numbers 27:18-23, where Moses laid hands on Joshua, whom God had chosen and equipped to become Moses' successor. What Moses had done by divine appointment, Joshua would continue by divine appointment. Done in the presence of all the people, Moses' laying hands on Joshua signified a transference of authority and power to exercise a leadership role among His people.

God had gifted the seven men for such tasks of ministry as were needed to resolve the painful crisis. On the basis of spiritual gifts already bestowed, the church made its selections. Then something that the apostles would otherwise have had to do would be done by others, whom God had chosen and equipped for the task. As Moses had laid his hands on Joshua before Israel, signifying a transference of role and authority, so the apostles laid their hands on the seven before the congregation. The church was expected to accept their administrative ministries as though they were being rendered by the apostles.

Often when we ordain deacons in our churches, we refer to this passage as though it recorded the institution of the office of deacon. Many Bible students do assume that Acts 6:1-7 records the origin of this office. The verb for "serve" appears in this passage in verse 3, and the noun *deacon* is from the same root word. Luke, however, never called the men "deacons." Indeed, the noun *deacons* never occurs in the Book of Acts. Instead in Acts 21:8 these men simply were called "the seven."

Only two of the seven, Stephen and Philip, figured in Luke's continuing account, and their ministries were not restricted to "serving tables." For Stephen was described as an effective Christian preacher, powerfully defending the claims of Christ (6:8—8:1). And Philip was doing the work of an evangelist with notable success in Samaria (8:4-40).

Renewed Growth (v. 7)

With the solving of the problem of internal dissension, Luke recorded the renewed growth of the church. As the Word of God spread, the number of the disciples in Jerusalem continued to increase. Furthermore, "a great many of the priests were becoming obedient to the faith" (v. 7).

Intensified Persecution (7:55—8:8; Focal: 7:55—8:8)

After Luke described overcoming the barrier of internal dissension in Acts 6:1-7, he turned immediately to Stephen's further ministry. Stephen was one of the seven (6:5). Obviously not limited to overseeing administrative tasks, he engaged in a ministry of the Word of God. He performed "great wonders and signs among the people" (6:8). However, some men from the "Synagogue of the Freedmen" took strong exception to Stephen's words, though they were unable to refute him (6:10). Thus frustrated, they secretly arranged to have men charge Stephen with speaking "blasphemous words against Moses and against God" (6:11). This aroused the people to the point that they eventually brought Stephen to the council, where they repeated and intensified their complaints (6:13-14).

To know more precisely the truth about the origin of their false charges would be interesting. What had Stephen proclaimed that had offended his hearers so intensely? That the accusations simply were trumped up without reference to what Stephen actually had said is unlikely. More likely, they were distortions. They charged that Stephen constantly was speaking out against the temple, claiming that Jesus would destroy it. (See similar charges against Jesus in Matt. 26:61; Mark 14:58.) Also, they accused him of opposing the law and altering the customs handed down by Moses (vv. 13-14).

Had Stephen perceived the temporary nature of the Mosaic law and the whole system of temple worship in the light of the redemptive work of Jesus Christ? Had Stephen seen that the old wineskins of a narrowed Jewish exclusivism never could contain the new wine of the gospel that God intended for all peoples?

One or both of these two attempts to probe behind the false charges is on target. The agitated Hellenists were unable to answer Stephen's arguments. Unsuccessful in refuting his words, they resorted to a devious expedient action to close his mouth, as frustrated traditionalism so often did and does. The deadly process eventually led to Stephen's murder; thus he became the first Christian martyr.

Stephen's Martyrdom (7:55—8:1)

Stephen was brought before the Jerusalem council, where the high priest asked him to respond to the serious charges brought against him. In what followed we have the longest speech recorded in the Book of Acts. Furthermore, it was not so much the kind of personal defense that might lead to acquittal as it was a defense of Christianity. Stephen recounted the history of God's gracious dealings with Israel from Abraham to Christ. The theme that pervaded Stephen's message was that Israel consistently had rejected the men whom God had chosen to bless her. First, he led up to the patriarchs' rejecting Joseph. They had sold their brother into Egyptian slavery (7:9). Then he continued his account up to Moses whom the quarreling Israelites rejected before his forty years in Midian (7:27). Also, Israel repudiated Moses at Mount Sinai, when their hearts longed to return to Egypt (7:39).

Stephen's account of Israel's record for rejecting God's chosen leaders reached its climax in the murder of Jesus Christ, the Righteous One (7:52). Just prior to this final indictment, Stephen described the members of Israel's highest court as "stiff-necked and uncircumcised in heart and ears" (7:51). With an extraordinary consistency, they always had resisted the Holy Spirit, even as their fathers had done. Their fathers had killed the prophets who had announced the coming of the Righteous One. Then when He came, the council had betrayed and murdered Him (7:52). Having received the law, as ordained by angels, these official keepers of the law had not kept it (7:53).

Such bold witnessing to God's truth in Christ yielded neither Stephen's acquittal nor Jewish converts. Instead rage mounted against Stephen (7:54). Then when he claimed to see "the heavens opened up and the Son of Man standing at the right hand of God" (7:56), his hearers could contain their fury no longer. Believing Stephen's words to be blasphemous, they covered their ears and rushed on him (7:57). They drove him out of the city and stoned him to death. While dying, Stephen called on the Lord to receive his spirit (7:59). Also, reminiscent of Jesus' prayer from the cross (Luke 23:34), he prayed for the forgiveness of his enemies (7:60).

Saul, at whose feet the stoners had laid their garments, "was in hearty agreement with putting him to death" (8:1).

In retrospect, we may make some comparisons between Peter's sermon at Pentecost (2:14-36) and Stephen's defense before the council (7:2-53). Both provided examples of Holy Spirit-empowered utterances. Both messages evoked a response, which is what such utterances are supposed to do. The converts were the evidence that Peter's listeners had heard him. The stones were Stephen's evidence that his listeners had heard him. The difference in the responses was not because Peter preached well and Stephen spoke poorly. Rather it lay in the hearers' responses: repentance and faith in one instance; rebellion and rejection in the other.

Most faithful witnesses will have occasions to experience variations of both Acts 2 and 7!

Driven from Jerusalem (8:1-8)

Devout men saw to it that Stephen had a decent burial, as believers throughout Jerusalem mourned his death. The atrocity, however, did not end or lessen the harassment of Christians in the city. Instead, it fanned the flames of a general persecution that was directed against all believers. Paul was particularly zealous in his efforts to destroy the church. He was a militant young Jewish believer. He disregarded the counsel of restraint that Gamaliel, his renowned teacher, urged (5:33-39). Going from house-to-house, he took believers from their homes and cast them into prison. In doing so, he thought he was accomplishing God's will (Gal. 1:13-14). Thus the church was scattered throughout Judea and Samaria.

The apostles however, remained in Jerusalem. Luke gave no explanation for their staying in Jerusalem. Those who were scattered by persecution, continued to preach the word. Among them was Philip, who like Stephen was one of the seven appointed to "serve tables" in Acts 6:5. He went to the city of Samaria (v. 5, or possibly a city in Samaria), where he proclaimed Christ to the people. Miracles of exorcism and healing attended his preaching, and many Samaritans believed. Luke recorded that "there was much rejoicing in that city" (v. 8).

A long history of prejudice and strife had marked relations between the Jews and Samaritans. To the Jews the Samaritans were the descendants of pagan colonists, moved into the land following Assyria's conquest of the Northern Kingdom of Israel in 722 B.C. However, the Samaritans maintained that they were the descendants of the Israelites who either had not been deported or had been repatriated. They had their own scroll of the Pentateuch, the only part of the Old Testament they accepted as Scripture. They had built their own temple atop Mount Gerizim, as a rival to the temple in Jerusalem. The Samaritan temple was destroyed in 129/128 B.C. by John Hyrcanus, a Jewish ruler. Jesus met this same rivalry while talking to the Samaritan woman at the well in Sychar (John 4:20).

Luke was able to describe Philip's ministry in the Samaritan city without any reference to this ancient prejudice (vv. 4-8). When news of the Samaritan revival reached the Jerusalem apostles, they sent Peter and John to look into the work (v. 14).

After laboring there for a time, they returned to Jerusalem, preaching the gospel to many Samaritan villages as they went (v. 25).

Philip and the Ethiopian Eunuch (8:26-40)

Previously Luke had recorded instances in which the gospel was preached to large crowds. For example, at Pentecost Peter preached to many Jews, and about three thousand were saved (2:41). Again, following the healing of the lame beggar, he preached to many Jews gathered in Solomon's portico, and the number of male converts reached about five thousand (4:4). Also, Luke recorded instances in which men witnessed boldly to the gospel in the presence of the Jewish council (4:8-12, 19-20; 5:29-32; 7:2-53).

Now we come to a passage in which there is a notable example of *personal* evangelism. In a one-on-one situation, Philip bore a Christian witness to an extraordinary person—the high-ranking eunuch from Ethiopia. The differences between the two men made the Ethiopian's conversion all the more remarkable.

The Ethiopian (vv. 26-28)

In the first-century Greco-Roman world, Ethiopia was designated as the land south of Egypt. It marked the limit of the known world in Africa. It was ruled by a succession of queen-mothers, who bore the dynastic title of Candace. The eunuch was an official in the Ethiopian court, having charge over all the queen's treasure.

At no point in the passage is his name given. Instead five times he is referred to simply as "a" or "the" eunuch. In the ancient world, for eunuchs (castrated males) to function as chamberlains in the women's quarters of royal households was not uncommon. This Ethiopian eunuch was a high official in a court ruled by a queen.

Questions frequently have been raised as to whether or not he was either a native Jew or a Gentile proselyte. That he was born a Jew is doubtful. Likely he was not a Gentile proselyte, for Deuteronomy 23:1 excluded eunuchs from religious privileges in Israel. Rather he probably was a God-fearer, a Gentile who attached himself to Judaism but stopped short of becoming a proselyte.

The eunuch had been to Jerusalem to worship, and now he was returning to Ethiopia in his chariot. As he rode along, he was reading from a Greek text of Isaiah 53:7-8 (v. 28).

The Encounter with Philip (vv. 29-40)

Not only does the Spirit empower Christians for service and inspire their utterance in all circumstances, but He also guides them. Evidence of this encouraging truth will be found elsewhere in the Book of Acts, but it is particularly vivid in verses 29-40. Several roads joined the communities of Judea and Samaria, but the angel of the Lord commanded Philip specifically, "Arise and go south to the road that descends from Jerusalem to Gaza" (v. 26). At that time and place, the eunuch was returning to Ethiopia with the fresh worship experiences of a Jewish festival still stirring in him. God's Spirit was working in both men, bringing together the man with the witness and the one needing it.

The men were total strangers to each other. Furthermore, significant cultural, economic, and possibly ethnic differences separated them. Yet where the Spirit of God was given freedom to work at both ends in evangelism, such barriers joyfully were overcome. Unknown to each other at the time that Philip received his directions, the two men were destined to become brothers in Christ forever. When Philip caught sight of the Ethiopian's chariot, the Spirit commanded him to go to it (v. 29). Running to catch up with it, Philip came close enough to hear the eunuch reading aloud Isaiah's prophecy of the Suffering Servant (Isa. 53:7-8). In a fine example of situational witnessing, Philip asked the eunuch if he understood what he was reading. And in a fine example of openness to the biblical revelation, the prominent Ethiopian confessed his ignorance and invited Philip to join him in the chariot (v. 31).

Prompted by the eunuch's question regarding the identity of the sufferer in the passage he had been reading, Philip "preached Jesus to him" (v. 35). For the great prophecy of Isaiah's Suffering Servant found its ultimate fulfillment in Jesus

Christ's self-sacrificing death on the cross.

Evidently Philip included the Lord's command to baptize converts, for when they came to a body of water, the eunuch exclaimed, "Look! Water! What prevents me from being baptized?" (v. 36). Possibly verse 37 reflects an early Christian practice, in which at the time of baptism the new convert made a public confession of his faith in response to a leading question. Both Philip and the eunuch went down into the water, where Philip baptized him (v. 38). As they came up out of the water, "the Spirit of the Lord snatched Philip away; and the eunuch saw him no more, but went on his way rejoicing" (v. 39).

Acts 8:40 provides a summary statement, describing Philip's continued evangelistic preaching in many cities "until he came to Caesarea." Evidently he settled there. We do not encounter Philip again until several years later in Acts 21:8-9. At that time, he was living in Caesarea with "four virgin daughters who were prophetesses" (21:9). They provided accommodations for Paul and his companions for several days, as they made their way to Jerusalem following the third missionary journey.

Lessons for Life from Acts 6:1—8:40

No church has a greater problem than when divisions plague its membership.—When persecution denied the early Christians their freedom to proclaim the gospel, they still thrived. Not even imprisonment or lashes could dampen their fervor and love for the Lord and each other. However, when they divided along cultural lines and watched each other very closely for suspected advantages, they created a grave threat to the gospel. Actually the gospel of Jesus Christ is the greatest love story ever told, and only love can tell it well. People who do not love may have the words right, but the vibrations will be wrong, and people feel vibrations while they hear words. Churches need to reflect the kind of love that God expressed for the whole world in His matchless gift of Jesus Christ, His only Son.

The Spirit of God can lead churches through their difficulties.—He did so in the Jerusalem church. First, the members need to meet together. People do not get together by staying apart. Then together, they have the privilege of seeking God's Spirit's sovereign leadership. His will must prevail rather than the will of any particular group. Not only will God's Spirit have a plan, but also He will equip those needed to implement it. Finally, the entire congregation has the responsibility for making the plan work. Concerted prayer must undergird the effort.

The Holy Spirit works at both ends in all evangelism.—That is, not only does He prepare the witnesses, He also prepares those who need to hear them. At Pentecost, the Holy Spirit empowered Peter to preach and also worked in the hearers to bring conviction. On the desert road from Jerusalem to Gaza, the same Spirit of God was preparing both Philip and the Ethiopian for their meeting. Indeed, in all our endeavors to bear an effective witness for Jesus Christ, the Holy Spirit goes before us.

Where Jesus Christ is experienced as Lord, great rejoicing prevails.—This is a common emphasis in Luke's account of Christian beginnings. When the council flogged and forbade the apostles to speak the name of Jesus, the apostles left the council "rejoicing that they had been considered worthy to suffer shame for His name" (5:41). When Philip proclaimed Christ to the Samaritans and they believed, "there was much rejoicing in that city" (8:8). When the Ethiopian eunuch was converted through his encounter with Philip, he emerged from the baptismal waters and "went on his way rejoicing" (8:39). Faith in Jesus Christ and deep well-springs of joy tend to thrive together.

1. Scripture quotations marked (RSV) are from the *Revised Standard Version of the Bible,* copyrighted 1946, 1952, © 1971, 1973 by the Division of Christian Education of the National Council of the Churches of Christ in the U.S.A., and used by permission.

2. Scripture quotations marked (Phillips) are from *The New Testament in Modern English,* translated by J. B. Phillips (New York: The Macmillan Co., 1958), 495.

3. Scripture quotations marked (NIV) are from the Holy Bible, *New International Version,* copyright © 1973, 1978, 1984 by International Bible Society.

4. Frank Stagg, *The Book of Acts* (Nashville: Broadman Press, 1955), 91.

Personal Learning Activities

1. List three barriers to the gospel which Dr. MacGorman says were overcome in this period? (1) _____ _____
   (2) _____ _____ (3) _____ _____ .

2. Underline the correct answer: One problem which arose in the early church was (1) dissension over the distribution of supplies to certain widows, (2) who would be elected president, (3) indecisive action on the part of the leaders (6:1-7).

3. List three qualities expected in the men selected to deal with the problem among the widows. (1) _____ _____ _____, (2) _____ ___ ___ _____, (3) _____ ___ _____ (6:3).

4. True _____ False _____ The apostles suggested that the congregation select seven men (6:2-6).

5. Two of the seven who were effective preachers were _____ and _____ (6:8—8:40).

6. True _____ False _____ Stephen's speech was accepted by the Jewish leaders (7:54-60).

7. What was the theme of Stephen's message? _____ _____ (7:1-53).

8. True _____ False _____ The messages by Peter (Acts 2) and Stephen (Acts 7) had different results.

9. A militant young Judaist who encouraged the stoning of Stephen was _____ of _____ (8:1).

10. Underline the correct answer. Philip had an effective ministry among (1) the Samaritans, (2) the Jewish priests, (3) the Roman soldiers (8:5-25).

11. Philip preached to crowds, but his encounter with the Ethiopian eunuch shows he was also an effective _____ _____ (8:26-39).

12. The subject of Philip's message to the eunuch was _____ as the Suffering Servant (8:35).

13. True _____ False _____ The eunuch showed he believed in Jesus by giving Philip a love offering.

14. True _____ False _____ After Philip left the eunuch, he had no more opportunities to preach the gospel.

15. Which of the four lessons which Dr. MacGorman listed in **Lessons for Life** is most helpful to you personally at this point in your life? _____

Answers: 1. Internal dissension, intensified persecution, individual differences. 2. (1). 3. Of good reputation, full of the Spirit, full of wisdom. 4. True. 5. Stephen, Philip. 6. False. 7. That Israel consistently rejected the men whom God chose to bless her. 8. True. 9. Saul, Tarsus. 10. (1). 11. Personal witness. 12. Jesus 13. False. 14. False. 15. Your choice.

4

Even to the Gentiles

Acts 9:1—12:25

The early chapters of Acts describe the triumphs and struggles of the first generation of believers in and around Jerusalem. On a hill called Golgotha outside the city wall, Jesus Christ, God's only Son, had died on a cross for the sins of a lost world. From a garden tomb He had emerged victorious over sin and death on the first Easter. The risen Lord had given instructions to His followers to stay in Jerusalem until they received "what the Father had promised" (1:4), namely, baptism with the Holy Spirit (1:5). This would equip them to bear witness at home and in distant places to God's gracious salvation through faith in His Son (1:8).

The early believer's waiting set the stage for the momentous events of the day of Pentecost, when many in Jerusalem heard the gospel and experienced its great power (2:1-42). During the days that followed God's Spirit worked mightily through the earliest believers' witnessing, and their numbers increased. Much of this growth took place in spite of the religious leaders' mounting hostility. Eventually, the hostility reached a climax in the stoning of Stephen (7:54-60). This desperate incident inflamed a widespread persecution of believers in Jerusalem and the believers scattered throughout Judea and Samaria (8:1).

Yet, wherever the persecutors drove the believers, the believers continued to witness faithfully to the gospel. As a result, a revival broke out in Samaria. Then Peter and John were sent from Jerusalem to confirm and participate in the revival (8:4-25). Also, a high-ranking official from Ethiopia took the gospel back to his distant home (8:26-39).

In Acts 9:1—12:25 the gospel extended even further from its Jerusalem base, and penetrated even to the Gentiles.

Particular attention will be given to the conversion of Saul of

Tarsus. Under divine appointment, he would become the apostle to the Gentiles (9:1-16). Even Peter, who was rigid in his Jewish traditionalism, was to have an effective ministry outside of Jerusalem (9:32-43). Eventually, God would compel him to overcome the prejudice that made entering a Gentile house unthinkable (10:1-48). Then when some unnamed believers from Cyprus and Cyrene came to Antioch and began to witness to Greeks as well as to the Jews, another exciting work developed (11:19-26). Indeed, the church in Antioch was destined to become the base for the mission to the Gentiles (13:1-3).

The Conversion of Saul: a Jewish Persecutor (9:1-16; Focal: 9:1-16)

We are not limited to Luke's account in Acts for our knowledge of the fierce persecution of the early Christians by Saul of Tarsus. The earliest references in Acts use the Hebrew name "Saul." Beginning in Acts 13:9, however, the Greek version of the name, "Paul," is introduced and used throughout the remaining chapters. We shall follow the text in our use of these names. Paul believed that he was serving God by destroying those who confessed Jesus Christ as Lord (see Gal. 1:13-14; 1 Cor. 15:9; Phil. 3:6; 1 Tim. 1:13).

Paul's testimony was complemented in the Book of Acts. Encountered first as the guardian of the robes of the men who stoned Stephen (7:58), Luke added the detail that "Saul was in hearty agreement with putting him to death" (8:1). Soon this young militant took the lead in a house-to-house search for Christians, dragging men and women alike off to prison (8:3).

Can you imagine a less likely prospect in all Jerusalem for God's choice as an apostle to the Gentiles?

Mission to Damascus (vv. 1-9)
Evidently some of the believers who had been driven from their homes in Jerusalem had sought refuge in Damascus. Many Jews lived in the city, and so there were several synagogues in the city.

Having learned about the flight of Christians to the Jewish community in Damascus, Saul was determined to bring them back as prisoners. He secured letters of extradition from the priestly leaders in Jerusalem, and headed for Damascus.

As Paul approached the city about midday, suddenly he was surrounded by a flashing light from heaven. Blinded by its overpowering brilliance, he fell to the ground. Then he heard a voice from heaven saying, "Saul, Saul, why are you persecuting Me?" (v. 4). And when Saul asked for identification, the exalted Lord replied, "I am Jesus whom you are persecuting" (v. 5).

The Lord in heaven identified Himself with His persecuted followers on the earth. Though exalted to a throne at the right hand of the Father, the Lord made Himself one with His people. Thus, the persecution of Christians became also a persecution of the Lord.

The men traveling with Saul heard a voice but saw no one (v. 7). And Saul, prostrate on the ground, was commanded to continue into the city, where he would be told what to do. He had traveled to Damascus to return Christians bound to Jerusalem. Instead, he was blinded by his confrontation with the exalted Christ. Then he was led into the city by the hand. For three sightless days he neither ate nor drank (v. 9).

But Saul prayed!

"A Chosen Instrument of Mine" (vv. 10-16)

And while Saul prayed, the Lord was giving a devout Christian named Ananias a disturbing assignment. He identified Saul of Tarsus and told Ananias where he was staying. Then he related how Saul had seen a vision in which a man named Ananias would lay hands on him, so that he might recover his sight (v. 12). But Saul's reputation as an infuriated persecutor of Christians had preceded him to Damascus. Thus Ananias was reluctant to have anything to do with him. Then the Lord said to Ananias, "Go, for he is a chosen instrument of Mine, to bear My name before the Gentiles and kings and the sons of Israel; for I will show him how much he must suffer for My name's sake" (vv. 15-16).

Two important observations need to be made: First, the exalted Christ had arrested the arch-persecutor of His people with the intention of making him an extraordinary witness to His name. Saul was to become the Lord's choice instrument. He would become an apostle to the Gentiles. He would plant churches in many places of the Mediterranean world and declare the gospel in the courts of rulers. His burden for his own kinsmen, the Jews, never would diminish (Rom. 9:1-5). And eventually, almost half of the 27 writings that constitute the New Testament were to come from his hand.

What a trophy of God's grace!

Second, being the Lord's chosen instrument carries no exemption from suffering for His name's sake. To the contrary, being chosen for service and suffering seem to be correlated; they are linked together. That Saul suffered unusual and extended hardships in fulfilling his calling is borne out in 2 Corinthians 11:23-33 (see 1 Cor. 4:9-13; Phil. 3:10). Yet much popular preaching persists in declaring that God's will is not that any of His people should suffer. If we have enough faith and no unconfessed sin in our lives, we are told that our health always will be robust and our bank accounts will be fat.

What a travesty of God's grace!

In verses 10-19, we learn that Ananias was obedient to the Lord's command. He went to Saul, described the Lord's instructions and promise, and baptized him (9:17-19). For some time in Damascus, Saul proclaimed that Jesus was the Son of God (9:19-22). Unable to refute Saul, the Jews who did not believe sought to kill him. However, he managed to escape through an opening in the city wall (9:23-25). When Saul tried to join the church in Jerusalem, he encountered grave suspicion (9:26). The members could not believe that one who had been so hostile toward them now could be one of their number.

However, Barnabas, whose generosity earlier had inspired the church (4:36-37), intervened in Saul's behalf. Not only did Saul join them but he also spoke out boldly in the name of the Lord (9:28). This incited the Hellenistic Jews' hostility. They tried to kill Saul (9:29). Thus, the brethren took him to the port of Caesarea, and sent him away to Tarsus, the place of his birth (9:30).

We will not hear of Saul again until Acts 11:25-30.

The Conversion of Cornelius: a God-fearing Gentile (10:1-48; Focal 10:1-16,25-29,34-43)

The last we heard of Peter he was returning with John to Jerusalem, after confirming the work in Samaria (8:25). Then Luke described some more of Peter's ministry outside of Jerusalem. Through him the risen Lord healed Aeneas, a paralytic who had been bedridden for eight years (9:32-35). Also, in Joppa, Tabitha (or Dorcas), a woman who had helped many people, was raised from the dead. In this study our primary interest centers in Peter's ministry to Cornelius, a Roman military officer in Caesarea (10:1-48). Here the gospel overcame the formidable barrier that separated Jews from Gentiles, as it reached out to all the people of the world.

Cornelius's Vision in Caesarea (vv. 1-8)

In verse 1, the man needing to hear the gospel was a Gentile—but no ordinary one. He was a centurion of what was called the Italian cohort or band (v. 1). A cohort was a tenth part of a Roman legion. Thus, a cohort numbered six hundred men. As a centurion, Cornelius commanded one hundred men. He was a man of authority, accustomed to giving orders and having others wait on him (v. 7).

Not only did Cornelius have an important rank in the Roman military, he also was "a devout man, and one who feared God with all his household, and gave many alms to the Jewish people, and prayed to God continually" (v. 2). Indeed, he was a God-fearer, a Gentile who was attracted to the monotheistic faith of Judaism and its high ethical standard. He was not a Gentile proselyte to the Jewish religion. Becoming a proselyte would have required circumcision, a purifying self-baptism, and likely the offering of a sacrifice.[1] Cornelius was a man of prayer and charitable deeds. Those under his command described him as "a righteous and God-fearing man well spoken of by the entire nation of the Jews" (v. 22).

One afternoon while praying (about 3:00 P.M.) Cornelius had a vision, in which an angel of God appeared and called him by name (v. 3). After commending his devotion and charity, the angel instructed Cornelius to send men to Joppa for Peter (vv.

4-6).

Soon Cornelius had two servants and a devout soldier on their way to Joppa, where Peter was staying with a tanner named Simon (vv. 7-8).

Vision in Joppa (vv. 9-16)

Around noon of the following day, Peter went up on the housetop to pray (v. 9). He became hungry, and while a meal was being prepared, he fell into a trance (v. 10). He had a vision of a great sheet coming down from heaven, filled with all kinds of animals, crawling creatures, and birds (vv. 11-12). A heavenly voice commanded Peter to rise, kill, and eat, but he refused. He reminded God that he never had broken the Levitical dietary code (Lev. 11) by eating anything unholy or unclean (v. 14). Rather than being commended for his strict observance of

the Jewish food laws, Peter was rebuked: "What God has cleansed, no longer consider unholy" (v. 15). Three times this vision was repeated before the object was taken up into the sky (v. 16).

While Peter was still pondering the meaning of the vision, Cornelius's messengers arrived at the gate of Simon's house. Having received assurance from the Spirit regarding them (vv. 19-20), Peter invited them to spend the night. The next day, accompanied by six Jewish Christians from Joppa, Peter and the messengers set out for Caesarea (v. 23).

Later in Jerusalem, Peter would have reason to be grateful for the supporting testimony of these six brethren (11:12).

A Gentile Household Converted (vv. 25-29,34-43)

A Prejudice Overcome (vv. 25-29).—The distance from Joppa to Caesarea was about 30 miles, and the following day Peter and his companions entered the city. Cornelius had invited several relatives and close friends into his home in anticipation of Peter's coming. When the apostle entered the house, Cornelius fell at his feet in a gesture of extraordinary respect or homage. Peter, however, was embarrassed and urged, "Stand up; I too am just a man" (v. 26). Such adoration is rightly reserved for God only—then and ever since.

For a devout Jew to enter the home of a Gentile was unthinkable. One reason for this was that Gentile food preparation made it difficult for a Jew to avoid ritual defilement. The meat served might have come from an animal regarded as unclean in the Levitical code. Or if clean, the animal might not have been slaughtered according to time-honored Jewish customs. Or maybe the meat was from an animal that had been offered in a pagan sacrifice, rendering it abhorrent to a devout Jew. Thus, it was better to avoid Gentile associations and hospitality altogether than to run the risk of ceremonial defilement. Even to enter a Gentile building or to handle articles belonging to Gentiles was to incur ritual uncleanness. (See John 18:28.)

With this kind of cultural background, Peter called Cornelius's attention to the unusual aspect of his coming (v. 28). Fortunately, Cornelius took no offense at Peter's blunt introduction. Rather, he related the account of his vision; he thanked

Peter for coming; and said, "Now then, we are all here present before God to hear all that you have been commanded by the Lord" (v. 33).

A Witness Given (vv. 34-43).—Once Peter moved beyond the barrier of his racial prejudice, he managed to bear a faithful witness. His words, "God has shown me that I should not call any man unholy or unclean" (v. 28), revealed his understanding of the vision in Joppa. Thus, he was able to begin his message to Cornelius's Gentile household by affirming that "God is not one to show partiality" (v. 34).

Then Peter gave what must have become an apostolic summary of Jesus Christ's ministry, beginning with His baptism and climaxing in His passion and resurrection. Anointed with the Holy Spirit and power at His baptism, Jesus had gone about doing good and healing all who were oppressed by the devil (v. 38). Yet His own people had "put Him to death by hanging Him on a cross" (v. 39). But "God raised Him up on the third day," thus reversing the verdict of those who condemned Him (v. 40). Moreover, after His resurrection, He appeared to those whom God had chosen beforehand to be His witnesses (v. 41). These He commissioned to preach the gospel to the people, declaring Jesus Christ to be the God-appointed Judge of the living and the dead (v. 42). The prophets bore witness that those who believed in Him would receive "forgiveness of sins" (v. 43).

A comparison of Peter's message here with his earlier messages at Pentecost (2:14-36), in Solomon's portico (3:12-26), and before the Sanhedrin (4:8-12,19; 5:29-32) is interesting. The earlier messages were delivered to Jewish hearers, but this one was delivered to Gentiles. Nevertheless the same essential thrust prevailed in all the messages. In each, references to Jesus' death on the cross were made. In each, Peter stated that God had raised Him up. And in each, Peter claimed that he was one of the witnesses of His resurrection.

Yet two differences may be noted: (1) For the Gentiles more details were given regarding Jesus' earthly ministry than in the earlier messages in a Jewish setting; (2) in speaking of those who put Jesus to death, Peter used "they" instead of "you" (v. 39).

Surely, verses 25-29,34-43 have value as an example of early

Christian preaching to those who were not Jews but who had some exposure to Judaism through synagogue worship.

Acts 10:44-48 describes the exciting conclusion to Peter's ministry in Cornelius' household. Before he finished preaching, the Holy Spirit fell on the hearers in great power. The Jewish believers from Joppa, who had accompanied Peter to Caesarea, were amazed that the Holy Spirit had come on the Gentiles as He had come on Jewish believers at Pentecost (v. 45). The new converts were speaking in tongues and exalting God (v. 46). Because of this evident outpouring of the Holy Spirit on the Gentile converts, they were baptized in the name of Jesus Christ (v. 48).

A splendid variety is evidenced by the Holy Spirit's work in the Book of Acts.

At Pentecost in Acts 2:37-42 the Holy Spirit apparently was received at the time of baptism. (See Acts 19:2.) No mention was made of laying on of hands, and nowhere did it say that the three thousand converts spoke in tongues.

In Samaria, in Acts 8:4-17, the Holy Spirit was received after baptism. The Samaritans had believed and been baptized when they heard Philip preach the gospel (v. 12). However, not until Peter and John had come from Jerusalem, had laid hands on them, and had prayed, did they receive the Holy Spirit. No specific manifestation of the Holy Spirit was described. Those who claim otherwise must resort to an inference based on the reaction of Simon the magician.

In Caesarea (Acts 10:44-48) the Holy Spirit was received before baptism. There was no laying on of hands. However, there was a specific manifestation of the Holy Spirit, namely "speaking with tongues and exalting God" (v. 46).

In view of these evidences of the variety in the working of the sovereign Holy Spirit in the Book of Acts, we would do well to avoid two errors. First, we must not isolate any passage and make it the norm while ignoring the others. Second, we must not glean certain features from each passage, creating a norm that would be true of none of them.

Indeed, no one should try to put God's sovereign Spirit in a box! We will do well to pray that God save us from such arrogance and presumption.

Even though there is variety in the Spirit's working, there are features that are common to each passage. First, each believer—whether Jew, Samaritan, or Gentile—heard the gospel of Jesus Christ and responded in faith. Second, each convert submitted to baptism. Third, each believer received the Holy Spirit, whether at the time of baptism, after baptism, or before. Fourth, all those who received the Holy Spirit experienced vibrant joy and evidences of new life. Sometimes these benefits were described in summary statements of the church's spiritual vitality, as in Acts 2:43-47. At other times they were described as specific manifestations of the Holy Spirit, as in Acts 10:46.

Peter Criticized in Jerusalem (11:1-3)

The news of Peter's witness and fellowship in Cornelius's home traveled quickly. Soon the Christian communities throughout Judea heard that the Gentiles also had received God's Word. This should have caused all believers to rejoice; however, for certain Jewish believers Peter's actions caused distress. When Peter returned to Jerusalem, they wasted little time confronting him with the charge, "You went to uncircumcised men and ate with them" (v. 3).

Peter responded to the challenge by detailing the events from the time of his vision in Joppa to the outpouring of the Holy Spirit on Cornelius and his household (vv. 4-15). Then after recalling the Lord's words about being baptized with the Holy Spirit, Peter climaxed his defense with a question. He asked, "If God therefore gave to them the same gift as He gave to us also after believing in the Lord Jesus Christ, who was I that I could stand in God's way?" (v. 17).

The question quieted further objection from the distressed Jewish believers. They allowed that God had "granted to the Gentiles also the repentance that leads to life" (v. 18).

However, the issue they raised about the inclusion of the Gentiles refused to be laid to rest. Later in Antioch, it provoked a controversy so big that it required a special conference with the leaders of the church in Jerusalem to resolve the issue (15:1-35).

The First Gentile Church (11:19-26)

Some of the believers scattered by the persecution that followed Stephen's death traveled northward to Phoenicia, Cyprus, and Antioch (v. 19; 8:4). In their witnessing, however, they spoke the Word to Jews only. The barrier separating Jews and Gentiles remained in place; thus, limiting the gospel outreach that God intended for all people. Eventually, some men of Cyprus and Cyrene who had come to Antioch began to witness to Greeks also (v. 20). God's blessings attended their efforts, so that many of them turned to the Lord (v. 21).

Reports of the success of the gospel in Antioch reached Jerusalem. This time not Peter and John but Barnabas was sent to evaluate and encourage this exciting new work among the Gentiles (v. 22). Described as a good man who was full of the Holy Spirit and faith (v. 24), Barnabas was a happy choice for the assignment. His outstanding example of generosity at an earlier time had commended him to the Jerusalem church (4:36-37). Also, he had been the one to intervene in Saul's behalf, when believers in Jerusalem had doubted Saul's conversion (9:27).

Arriving in Antioch, Barnabas rejoiced as he witnessed God's grace at work among the Gentiles. He encouraged the new converts to remain true to the Lord (v. 23). Indeed, so many Gentiles were being won to the Lord, that the work load strained Barnabas' capacity. At this juncture Saul came to mind, and Barnabas went to Tarsus to look for him (v. 25). When he found Saul, Barnabas persuaded him to return with him to Antioch. Barnabas and Saul served together in Antioch for the next year (v. 26). Luke added the detail that "the disciples were first called Christians in Antioch" (v. 26).

Not only was the church in Antioch the first Gentile church, but also it was destined to become the missionary base for the evangelization of regions around the Aegean Sea. Thus relatively early in Christian history, Jerusalem gave way to Antioch as the strong center for the propagation of the gospel to the world.

In the remaining passages of Acts through chapter 12, Luke described: (1) the famine relief offering sent from Antioch to Jerusalem under the supervision of Barnabas and Saul (11:27-

30); (2) the martyrdom of James, the brother of John, under King Agrippa I (12:1-2); (3) the subsequent arrest and miraculous deliverance of Peter (12:3-19); (4) the death of King Agrippa I in Caesarea following a political oration (12:20-23); (5) Barnabas and Saul's return to Antioch, accompanied by John Mark (12:24-25).

Lessons for Life from Acts 9:1—12:25

Saul's conversion encourages us to persist in prayer for those who are hostile to the gospel.—No wonder that Ananias in Damascus was reluctant to carry out the Lord's instructions to minister to Saul. And no wonder that Jerusalem believers were reluctant to receive Saul into their fold. By his own admission, he had tried to destroy the church of God. Yet, by God's grace he was converted while on a persecution mission to Damascus. Then he became the greatest missionary of all time.

Prejudice in any form is a tragic obstacle to the progress of the gospel.—It gives the lie to the gospel that proclaims the love of God for all people. Did the Spirit of God have a harder time getting Peter to bear a gospel witness to a Gentile than He had in getting Cornelius ready to receive it?

The Holy Spirit is sovereign in all His work.—In the Book of Acts the Holy Spirit empowers, guides, inspires, sustains, and equips Christians for telling the gospel. But He works according to His sovereign will and not by any fixed formulas that we may seek to impose on Him. And the greatest evidence in Acts of the presence and power of the Holy Spirit in a believer's life is bold witnessing to God's redeeming grace in Jesus Christ, His Son.

---

1. See F. F. Bruce, *The Book of Acts,* (Grand Rapids, MI: WM. B. Eerdmans Pub. Co., 1988), 58.

Personal Learning Activities

1. True _____ False _____ Saul believed that he was serving God by destroying those who confessed Jesus as Lord (8:1).
2. Underline the correct answer. Although Jesus had been exalted to the right hand of the Father, (1) His followers never

could be hurt (2) to persecute Christians was to persecute Him (3) everyone who heard the gospel was saved (9:4).

3. When Ananias was reluctant to minister to Saul, God informed him that Saul was a _____ _____ , to bear His name before _____ , _____ , and _____ (9:15).

4. List four things which Ananias did in response to God's instruction: (1) _____ (2) _____ , (3) _____ (4) _____ (9:17-19).

5. True _____ False _____ After his conversion, Saul was received by the believers in Jerusalem only because Barnabas stood up on Saul's behalf (9:26-30).

6. Under Peter's ministry described in Acts 9—10, Aeneas was _____, Tabitha (Dorcas) was _____ _____ _____, and Cornelius, a Gentile, was _____.

7. List 6 facts about Cornelius before his conversion. (1) _____ (2) _____ (3) _____ (4) _____ (5) _____ (6) _____ .

8. True _____ False _____ When Peter refused to eat unclean animals shown him in a vision, God commended him for not compromising his convictions (10:15-16).

9. True _____ False _____ When Peter explained that coming to a Gentile was unusual, Cornelius got mad (10:28-33).

10. Peter proved he had overcome his racial prejudice when he said: " _____ " (10:34-35).

11. True _____ False _____ Peter preached basically the same gospel to Gentiles which he preached to Jews.

12. True _____ False _____ The gift of the Holy Spirit follows the same pattern in each experience in Acts.

13. When Peter told the believers in Jerusalem about the conversion of Cornelius, they glorified God for granting the Gentiles _____ that leads to life (11:18).

14. The first Gentile church was established at _____ in Syria with _____ and _____ the first pastors (11:19-30).

Answers: 1. True. 2. (2). 3. Chosen instrument, Gentiles, kings, Israel. 4. Went to Saul, told Saul about the Lord, laid hands on him, baptized him. 5. True. 6. Healed, raised from death, saved. 7. Gentile, military man, devout, feared God, gave alms, prayed. 8. False. 9. False. 10. "God is not one to show partiality". 11. True. 12. False. 13. The repentance. 14. Antioch, Barnabas, Saul.

5

The Mission to Asia Minor and the Jerusalem Council

Acts 13:1—15:35

This chapter will cover some of the most important events recorded in the Book of Acts. At its outset in Acts 13:1-3, we join a small group of church leaders in Antioch for a solemn meeting. Heretofore, the widening reach of the gospel to the Samaritans and Greeks had come largely as a result of the scattering of Christians by persecution. As they were driven from their homes in Judea, believers carried a gospel witness to the lands in which they sought refuge. But now in an orderly assembly of fasting and prayer in the Antioch church, the sovereign Spirit of God launched a movement to evangelize the world. Even to this day, we gain our basic strategy for world missions from what took place in this epochal meeting.

Also, in this chapter we will join the team of Barnabas, Saul, and John Mark for the first of the three missionary journeys recorded in Acts. The story relates dramatic episodes of travel, confrontation, desertion, opportunity, success, jealousy, hostility, courage, and threat of death. Yet when Barnabas and Saul eventually returned to their home base in Antioch, they had exciting experiences to share as to how God "had opened a door of faith to the Gentiles" (14:27).

Then in the midst of the thriving work in Antioch, a grave threat arose in the form of a Judaic controversy. This was far more serious than the earlier dissension in Jerusalem regarding discrimination against the widows of the Hellenistic Jews (6:1-6). This threat challenged the essence of the gospel as a gospel of grace rather than law. Earlier some of the "circumcised" party in the Jerusalem church had challenged Peter for entering and eating in the home of the Gentile Cornelius (11:2-3). They were silenced temporarily by Peter's account of the Holy Spirit's guidance and authentication of his actions in Caesarea (11:18). However, they did not remain quiet long. Soon some of their number showed up in Antioch. They insisted that Gentiles could not be saved apart from circumcision (15:1). So intense was the ensuing controversy, that it required a top level meeting of church leaders in Jerusalem to address the issue. This urgent convocation commonly has been designated the Jerusalem Council (15:1-35).

Birth of the Gentile Mission (13:1-4)

To attempt great works for God does not take large numbers of people; however, it does require persons who are committed to His work. In His earthly ministry, Jesus had chosen as apostles twelve men to share His life and mission most intimately. And there were only about 120 followers gathered in the upper room in Jerusalem on the eve of Pentecost (1:15).

Still fewer people were present in the extraordinary prayer meeting in Antioch, which was so important for world missions. Only five of these prophets and teachers were named: "Barnabas, and Simeon who was called Niger, and Lucius of Cyrene, and Manaen who had been brought up with Herod the tetrarch, and Saul" (v. 1). Of these only two, Barnabas and Saul, appear again in Acts. Since Simeon was given a Latin nickname **Niger,** meaning *black,* some scholars have assumed that he had a dark complexion. Some have suggested that he may have come from Africa.[1] Lucius of Cyrene likely was numbered among the Cyrenians in Antioch who first preached the gospel to the Greeks (11:20). And Manaen was described as one who had been reared with Herod Antipas, son of Herod the Great and tetrarch of Galilee and Perea from 4 B.C. to A.D. 39. Bruce explains, "The title 'foster-brother' was given to boys of the same age as royal princes, who were brought up with them at court."[2]

How strange that one of these foster-brothers of Herod is known to us as a Christian leader in Antioch, while Herod is known as the executioner of John the Baptist (Matt. 14:1-12)! Also, Herod and his soldiers subjected Jesus to cruel mockery during his trial in Jerusalem (Luke 23:8-12).

While Barnabas, Simeon, Niger, Lucius, and Manaen were worshiping the Lord and fasting in Antioch, the Holy Spirit said, "Set apart for Me Barnabas and Saul for the work to which I have called them" (v. 2). And after fasting and prayer, they laid their hands on Barnabas and Saul, and sent them away (v. 3). Here the laying on of hands was in recognition of something that the Holy Spirit already had done. It did not impart to Barnabas and Saul a qualification that they did not have. Rather, as stated by I. Howard Marshall, the laying on of hands was "an act of blessing in which the church associated itself with them and commended them to the grace of God (14:26)."[3] Later they would report to the entire church what God had done through them on their mission (14:27).

From Acts 13:1-4, we may discern the three indispensable factors in Christian world missions. First, there must be a recognition of the Holy Spirit's leadership in every aspect of missionary endeavor. His sovereignty must be acknowledged in the calling, equipping, and directing of those who participate in world evangelism. The task simply does not yield to a lesser power. Second, there needs to be a home base, like the church in Antioch, to provide both spiritual and material support for those who go. The greatness of any church, large or small, may be determined by the proportion of its energies and resources that are committed to winning a lost world to Jesus Christ. Congregations that spend all but a pittance of their resources on themselves are missing churches rather than mission churches. And third, there must be believers like Barnabas and Saul, who in obedience to the Spirit's call and direction will go near and far with the good news of the gospel.

Mission to Asia Minor (13:5—14:28; Focal: 13:13-14,51—14:2,5-7,19-28)

Actually Barnabas, Saul, and John Mark's first destination was the island of Cyprus. This was the native home of Barnabas. From the Syrian port city of Seleucia the missionaries sailed approximately 130 miles to Salamis, the main harbor on the island. There they proclaimed the gospel in the Jewish synagogues (13:5).

Then they made their way to Paphos, the capital city located at the western end of the island. The Roman proconsul, Sergius Paulus, had his official residence there. He became a believer when he saw Elymas, his court magician, stricken with temporary blindness because of his opposition to the gospel (13:9-12).

In Acts 13:9 the name "Paul" was used instead of "Saul," and it will continue throughout the rest of Acts. Also, in Acts 13:13 Luke wrote "Paul and his companions" instead of "Barnabas and Saul" as earlier. Apparently during the time in Cyprus, Paul emerged as the leader of the first missionary team.

Following the campaign in Cyprus, the missionaries sailed to Perga in Pamphylia, where surprisingly John Mark deserted them and returned to Jerusalem (13:13). Thereafter Luke described the evangelization of the southern part of the Roman province of Galatia. Amidst many trying circumstances, churches were planted and strengthened there.

John Mark's Desertion (13:13-14)

Luke simply recorded John Mark's abandonment of the mission tour without offering a clue as to the reason for it. And as is usual, where the Bible has remained silent, many writers have not done likewise. Thus several explanations have been proposed: (1) Barnabas was his cousin, and John Mark resented the fact that Paul had taken over as the leader; (2) he had second thoughts about Paul's views regarding the admission of Gentiles into the church; (3) he became uneasy about the possible dangers of travel in a strange territory; (4) he attributed the failure of the recent preaching in Cyprus to the lack of a manual for instructing new converts; thus, he returned to Jerusalem to prepare one—our Gospel of Mark; and (5) he was homesick for Jerusalem. All these are mere guesses with varying degrees of credibility.

However, we may be sure that John Mark's decision to leave was not an unanimous decision. Paul regarded it as a desertion and resented it. Later, at the beginning of the second missionary journey, Paul refused Barnabas' request that his young kinsman be given a second chance. Indeed, the contention between them in the matter became so sharp that the veteran missionary team split and went their separate ways (15:36-41).

The Evangelization of Southern Galatia (13:51—14:28)

After leaving Perga, Paul and Barnabas visited several places in the Roman province of Galatia. Galatia is used here in the provincial sense, not in the territorial sense.

Antioch of Pisidia and Iconium (13:51—14:2,5-7).—From Perga in Pamphylia, Paul and Barnabas traveled north through the Taurus mountain range to Antioch near the border of Pisidia. It was a civil and military center, with an altitude of thirty-six hundred feet, and it enjoyed status as a Roman colony.[4]

On the sabbath Paul and Barnabas worshiped in the synagogue, and were invited to speak. Paul responded with one of the major speeches recorded in the Book of Acts (13:16-41). Addressing a mixed audience of Jews and God-fearing Gentiles, he traced God's dealings with Israel from the Exodus to the enthronement of David. Then he proclaimed Jesus as the One in whom the promises made to David had their fulfillment. From this affirmation he proceeded to summarize the account of Jesus' ministry. Paul began with Jesus' baptism and climaxed with His crucifixion and resurrection. Then he ended his message with a warning against neglect.

In Paul's recital of Hebrew history as a background for proclaiming Jesus as Savior, he followed a pattern similar to Stephen's defense before the Jerusalem Council (7:2-53). In his climactic rehearsal of the crucifixion, resurrection, and appearances of Jesus to His followers, Paul reiterated themes central to Peter's messages (2:22-36). Indeed, Paul's message in Pisidian Antioch provided an example of his preaching in a synagogue of Jews who lived in a Gentile territory.

At first the worshipers in Antioch of Pisidia heard Paul gladly, inviting him and Barnabas to return the following sabbath. But eventually, the unbelieving Jews spearheaded a persecution that forced them to leave the district. As they left for Iconium, they shook the dust off their feet in a gesture of abandonment (13:51).

The pattern of initial success and eventual persecution prevailed in the evangelization of Iconium (14:1-2). Believers in both cities were left behind, but Paul and Barnabas were forced to flee to Lystra and Derbe, cities of Lycaonia (14:5-7).

Lystra and Derbe (14:19-20).—Acts 14:8-18 describes Paul's healing of a man lame from birth in Lystra. When the pagan inhabitants saw the healing miracle, they exclaimed in the Lycaonian language that the gods had come down to them in the forms of men (v. 11). They called Barnabas, Zeus, and Paul, Hermes, because he was the primary spokesman (v. 12). Almost before the apostles could discern the excited people's intentions, preparations were under way to offer a sacrifice to them (v. 13). When Paul and Barnabas realized what was about to take place, they tore their garments in a gesture of abhorrence and sought to dissuade the crowd. Their message in verses 15-17 is the first recorded Christian message to a pagan audience. Of necessity, it differed considerably from the approach Paul made, while addressing Jews and God-fearers in a synagogue in Pisidian Antioch (13:16-41).

In a synagogue, a common heritage of monotheistic faith and experience prevailed. Also, the Old Testament was a commonly accepted religious authority. Thus when preaching in a synagogue, Paul regularly sought to prove from the Scriptures that Jesus was the Christ, God's Anointed One or Messiah.

None of these advantages was present in the streets of a pagan city like Lystra. Thus Paul and Barnabas sought to bear a witness by appealing to God's revelation through nature, a revelation of His handiwork. (See Rom. 1:20.)

Eventually, the Jews from Pisidian Antioch and Iconium came to Lystra and stirred up the people's wrath against the apostles. They stoned Paul and dragged him out of the city, thinking that they had killed him (v. 19). However, he revived, returned to the city, and left the following day for Derbe (v. 20).

Return to Antioch of Syria (14:21-28).—From Derbe, Paul and Barnabas could have taken a direct route back to their home base in Antioch of Syria. However, they chose to retrace their steps through Lystra, Iconium, and Pisidian Antioch, strengthening the newly founded churches along the way (vv. 21-22). In order to stabilize the churches in their troubled circumstances, they appointed elders in each congregation (v. 23). After they prayed and fasted with the churches, they made their way through Perga to the Mediterranean port of Attalia (v. 25). From there they sailed to Antioch of Syria, where they reported to the church what God had done with them in taking the gospel to the Gentiles.

The Jerusalem Council (15:1-21; Focal: 15:1-21)

Following their return from the first missionary journey (13:4—14:28), Paul and Barnabas remained a long time with the disciples in Antioch. There was much for which to thank God in planting new churches in the cities of southern Galatia. Furthermore, God's Spirit was working mightily in Antioch, and the church was thriving. Even the touchy issue of the table fellowship of Jewish believers with Gentile converts was for a while overcome. Galatians 2:12 describes a time in Antioch when Peter and the other Jewish Christians regularly ate with the Gentiles.

This progress in the gospel, however, suffered a drastic setback. The coming of "certain men from James" (Gal. 2:12) is a possible background to the Acts 15 meeting. Made apprehensive by their presence and claims, Peter began to withdraw from table fellowship with the Gentiles. His leadership role and example caused other Jewish Christians to segregate themselves also. Even Barnabas, who from the beginning had been in the forefront of gospel endeavors among the Gentiles, was caught up in this hypocritical lapse (Gal. 2:13). And faithfulness to the gospel forced on Paul the unpleasant task of rebuking Peter publicly (Gal. 2:14).

According to this description, the events of Galatians 2 preceded those recorded in Acts 15. Of course, some other scholars view Galatians 2 in a different light and conclude that the incidents and meetings in Acts 15 and Galatians 2 are not the same.

The Issue (vv. 1-5)

"Unless you are circumcised according to the custom of Moses, you cannot be saved" (v. 1). This was the distressing pronouncement unloaded on the predominantly Gentile church in Antioch by the presumptuous emissaries from Jerusalem. They insisted that the Gentiles could not be saved by faith in Jesus as God's Messiah only. To their faith in Him, they would have to add circumcision, the sign of the covenant community of Israel (Gen. 17:9-14), and all that it entailed for the devout Jew. As the rite of circumcision was required of Gentile proselytes to Judaism, so it had to be required of Gentile converts to Christianity.

Clearly the issue was religion as grace or law. This choice seems to designate the ultimate alternatives in religion at any time. In religion based on grace, God is the *achiever* and man the grateful *receiver* of what God has done. Whereas in religion by law, man is the *achiever* and God the grateful *receiver* of what man has done. Faith is the inevitable accompaniment of religion as grace, even as works are the inevitable accompaniment of religion as law. Grace shifts the center of man's glorying from self to God, whereas works prompt glorying in self-achievement.

The essence of religious legalism is that it is forever placing a sign above the cross on which Jesus Christ died for the sins of the world with the words inscribed, "Necessary, but not enough!" To faith in Him as Savior and Lord, you must add something. In the Judaic controversy in Antioch, the thing to be added to the law was circumcision and obedience. But this was only one historical manifestation of the pervasive and continual threat of religious legalism to the gospel of God's grace. Ironically even the Christian ordinances of baptism and the Lord's Supper can be perverted legalistically so as to constitute a threat to the gospel of grace.

No wonder that Paul and Barnabas engaged the Judaizing brothers from Jerusalem in vigorous debate, but apparently to no avail. Eventually the decision was made that Paul, Barnabas, and others should go to Jerusalem for a discussion of the issue with leaders there (v. 2). Passing through Phoenicia and Samaria on the way, they told the churches about the conversion of the Gentiles (v. 3). Understandably their sympathies in the controversy would rest more with Paul and Barnabas than with the ultra-traditional faction in the Jerusalem church.

Arriving in Jerusalem, the delegation from Antioch was given a fine reception and hearing by the church and its leaders (v. 4). But "certain ones of the sect of the Pharisees who had believed" were there to repeat the demand, "It is necessary to circumcise them, and to direct them to observe the Law of Moses" (v. 5).

The Deliberations and Conclusion (vv. 6-21)
Peter's Message (vv. 6-11).—After the apostles and elders had debated the issue at length, Peter arose to speak. First, he related how in the early days God had chosen him to preach the gospel to the Gentile household of Cornelius in Caesarea (v. 7). He made a particular reference to God's witness to the Gentiles in "giving them the Holy Spirit, just as He also did to us" (v. 8). Obviously the likeness that linked Pentecost (Acts 2) and Caesarea (Acts 10) was the pouring forth of the Holy Spirit as God's gift to believing hearers. For God made no distinction between Jews and Gentiles on those occasions, because He cleansed the hearts of all through faith (v. 9).

Then Peter argued that any attempt to put the yoke of the law on the Gentile converts' necks would be to put God to the test (v. 10). After all, God already had borne witness to them by pouring out the Holy Spirit on them. Also, Peter acknowledged that the Jews had not been able to bear the yoke of the law that the Pharisaic faction was so ready to lay on Gentile believers (v. 10).

Peter concluded by affirming the Christian message as a gospel of God's grace for all (v. 11). God was God of Jews and Gentiles alike, and He reconciled both to Himself through the same gospel of grace.

Peter's utterance was true and timely, and it contributed to a positive resolution of the crisis. It prepared the way for Paul and Barnabas to relate more of the "signs and wonders God had done through them among the Gentiles" (v. 12).

James's Message (vv. 12-21).—However, the climactic message at the Jerusalem Council was delivered by James, the Lord's brother. James evidently had risen to a position of preeminence in the Jerusalem church. And he made the proposal that eventually found favor with them all.

First, James summarized Peter's message regarding God's call to the Gentiles, and confirmed it with a citation from "the Prophets" (v. 15). This term designated all the written prophetic material in the Old Testament. The specific reference was to the Septuagint or Greek version of Amos 9:11-12. Obviously the inclusion of the Gentiles among the people of God in the Septuagint version of the passage supported James's argument. Thus he advised the council not to "trouble those who are turning to God from among the Gentiles" (v. 19). The demand for the circumcision of Gentile converts and their strict adherence to Jewish laws must be denied.

As in all successful mediation between factions, however, not all the yielding must come from one side. Gentile converts needed to become more sensitive about certain pagan practices that were particularly offensive to devout Jewish believers. Thus James proposed next "that we write to them that they abstain from things contaminated by idols and from fornication and from what is strangled and from blood" (v. 20).

This request dealt primarily with matters relating to ritual defilement. For a Jew to eat meat that had been offered in idolatrous worship was regarded as sacrilegious. Furthermore, Jewish scruples forbade the eating of blood or meat from which the blood had not been drained properly. Also, Jewish communities generally deplored the sexual degradations that pervaded pagan society.

The Gentile sensitivity that James called for was particularly appropriate in view of the widespread Jewish communities of the ancient world. Synagogues were in many cities where the law of Moses was read every sabbath (v. 21).

All those present approved James's proposal. To implement it, they prepared a letter for the Gentile churches of Syria and Cilicia, containing the council's decision (vv. 23-29). It expressly discredited those who originally had given the impression in Antioch that they had come as emissaries of the Jerusalem church (v. 24). In addition, the church selected two of its leading members, Judas called Barsabbas and Silas, to accompany Paul, his companions, and the letter back to Antioch.

When the men returned, the church gathered for a report of the conference. The letter was read, and all rejoiced and were encouraged (v. 31). Judas and Silas added their words of confirmation and testimony (v. 32). Then they returned to Jerusalem in peace (v. 33). Once more Paul and Barnabas were able to devote their energies to evangelism rather than controversy. Evangelism is always the more suitable expression of Christian commitment (v. 35).

Lessons for Life from Acts 13:1—15:35

World evangelism is every Christian's privilege and responsibility.—Under the guidance of the Holy Spirit, men and women are still being called to mission fields at home and abroad. Those who are not called to go are called to provide the spiritual and material support that is essential to a vigorous mission enterprise.

Wise proclamation of the gospel will take note of the varying backgrounds and circumstances of the hearers.—A synagogue service in Pisidian Antioch afforded some advantages for witnessing that were not present in the open streets of a pagan city like Lystra. Paul recognized the differences in these settings and witnessed accordingly.

Religious legalism persists as a threat to the preaching of the gospel.—Legalism is a stifling smog that pollutes the pure air of God's redeeming grace. Moreover, some who are evangelical in their understanding of conversion tend to become legalistic in their understanding of Christian growth. However, the good news of the gospel is that we are *saved* by grace; we *grow* by grace; and we are *endowed* by grace for Christian service.

In religious controversy, God's people must move toward each other.—For any faction to assume an immovable stance that requires all concessions to be made by others will not do. Sometimes believers seem to mistake a mean and intransigent spirit for strength of conviction. Not all flexibility is a compromise of the faith, and not all rigid action is holy!

1. T.C. Smith, "Acts," *The Broadman Bible Commentary,* vol. 10 (Nashville: Broadman Press, 1970), 79.

2. F. F. Bruce, *Book of Acts* (Grand Rapids, MI: Wm. B. Eerdmans Pub. Co., 1988), 245.

3. I. Howard Marshall, *The Acts of the Apostles, The Tyndale New Testament Commentaries* (Grand Rapids: Wm. B. Eerdmans Pub. Co., 1980), p. 216.

4. See W. M. Ramsay, *St. Paul the Traveler and the Roman Citizen* Nashville: Broadman Press, 1979), pp. 91-97.

5. See F. F. Bruce, *Book of Acts,* 284.

Personal Learning Activities

1. In an assembly of prayer and fasting in the church at Antioch, "the sovereign Spirit of God launched a movement to _____ _____ _____ " (13:1-4; see also paragraph 1 of this chapter).

2. List three "indispensable factors in Christian world missions" discussed by Dr. MacGorman: _____ , _____ , _____ .

3. Cyprus was a good place to begin because it was the home of _____ (13:4; 4:36).

4. True _____ False _____ Paul and Barnabas were glad when John Mark decided to return to Antioch (13:13; 15:36-41).

5. True _____ False _____ Paul's sermon at Pisidian Antioch, in which he spoke of God's dealings with Israel and of Jesus' death and resurrection, was an example of his preaching to dispersed Jews (13:16-41).

6. The response of Paul's hearers followed a pattern of initial _____ and eventual _____ (13:42-52).

7. Match the following:

_____ (1) Antioch of Syria   A. Where Paul was stoned.

_____ (2) Perga in Pamphylia   B. Where John Mark left them.

_____ (3) Lystra   C. Gentile question debated.

_____ (4) Jerusalem Council   D. Missionary journey started.

8. In his sermon at Lystra, the first recorded Christian message preached to a pagan audience, Paul's approach was _____ (14:15-17).

9. Paul chose to retrace the route of the first missionary journey in order to _____ (14:21-22).

10. Underline the correct answer. The issue at the Jerusalem Conference (Acts 15) was (1) whether Peter should be pastor of the Jerusalem church, (2) who would be the next missionaries, (3) whether or not Gentiles could be saved without becoming Jewish proselytes.

11. Dr. MacGorman said that salvation by grace through faith makes God the _____ and man the _____; salvation by law through works makes God the _____ and man the _____.

12. The council at Jerusalem accepted James's proposal that _____ be accepted as true believers and that they be asked to abstain from _____ , _____ , _____ , and _____ (15:19-20).

Answers: 1. Evangelize the world. 2. The Holy Spirit's leadership, a home base of support, willing believers. 3. Barnabas. 4. False. 5. True. 6. Success, persecution. 7. (1) D, (2) B, (3) A, (4) C. 8. God's revelation through nature. 9. Strengthen the churches. 10. (3). 11. Achiever, receiver, receiver, achiever. 12. Gentiles, idols, fornication, things strangled, blood.

73

6

The Gospel's Spread to New Areas

Acts 15:36—18:28

In the days following the Jerusalem Council, Paul and Barnabas continued to teach and preach in Antioch. However, the time came when Paul's concern for the churches founded on the first missionary journey led him to propose to Barnabas a return visit. Barnabas was willing but wanted to take again John Mark, his cousin. Paul had not forgotten Mark's earlier desertion in Pamphylia, and refused to start a second journey with one who had failed to endure the rigors of the first trip. So intense was their disagreement that they broke up a lengthy missionary partnership and went their separate ways.

Luke's account recorded nothing about the return of Barnabas and John Mark to Cyprus (15:39). Rather, Luke focused on Paul and Silas as they began the second missionary journey. Silas was one of the two Jerusalem delegates formerly sent to Antioch (15:22). This time, Paul not only revisited the churches established earlier but also spread the gospel to new areas, even into Europe.

Once again, we will be able to discern certain features of Paul's missionary strategy: (1) He usually sought to establish a beachhead for the gospel by preaching first in the synagogues. Among the God-fearing Gentiles attached to the synagogues, he particularly enjoyed some success. This, of course, explained the Jews' jealousy. They had hoped that many of the Gentiles would become proselytes to Judaism. (2) He majored on planting churches in the cities, such as Philippi, Thessalonica, Berea, Athens, Corinth, and Ephesus. From these urban centers the gospel could spread into the surrounding areas. (3) He remained sensitive to the varying cultural contexts of his witness. Paul's message before the Areopagus in Athens was not the same as his message in a synagogue in Thessalonica or Berea, though his witness remained the same.

The material chosen for chapter 6 actually includes more than the events of the second missionary journey (15:36—18:22). It encompasses the beginning of the third journey, containing a brief account of Apollos's ministry in Ephesus and Corinth (18:23-28).

From Antioch to Philippi
(15:40—16:40; Focal: 15:40—16:15,23-34)

Rift with Barnabas (15:40-41)

The break-up of Paul and Barnabas is sad. For so many years, they had been leaders and co-laborers in preaching the gospel to the Gentiles. Barnabas was the one who had intervened with the Jerusalem church in Paul's behalf, when he returned to the city following his conversion (9:27). Also, Barnabas was the Jerusalem church's choice to investigate the new work among the Gentiles in Antioch (11:22-24). At the time, no better choice could have been made. Indeed, as the gospel progressed in Antioch, Barnabas made a trip to Tarsus to enlist Paul's help (11:25). For an entire year they worked side-by-side in Antioch.

Later during a famine the church in Antioch had placed them in charge of a relief offering to the poor believers in Judea (11:29-30). And just think of the experiences they had shared on the first journey. Who could forget their confrontation with Elymas the magician in the official residence of the Roman procurator in Paphos (13:15-52)? Then there were the anxious days of Paul's illness in Galatia (Gal. 4:13-14). First they were heard in Pisidian Antioch and then hounded out of the city (13:15-52). The pattern was repeated in Iconium (14:1-5). Originally received as gods in Lystra, adoration soon became violence, as Paul was stoned and dragged outside the city for dead (14:8-19).

Back in Antioch, Paul and Barnabas had debated vigorously against those from Jerusalem who were demanding that the Gentile converts be circumcised as an essential to salvation

(15:1). And when the crisis could not be resolved on a local level, the church had sent them as its primary delegates to the Jerusalem Council (15:2-35).

With so broad a base of missionary partnership, the inclusion or exclusion of John Mark by itself hardly seems to account for the split. Later Paul came to appreciate John Mark (see Col. 4:10; Philem. 24; 2 Tim. 4:11). Also, in 1 Cor. 9:6, written later, Paul referred to Barnabas as his missionary partner.

Possibly Paul's public rebuke regarding the table fellowship fiasco in Antioch left some wounds that never had healed completely (Gal. 2:11-14). At any rate, the foremost missionary team quarreled and separated, and anytime Christian leaders part company on other than friendly terms it is sad.

Paul's choice of Silas as his missionary partner enjoyed at least two advantages: (1) He was an authorized representative of the Jerusalem church to Antioch in support of the Council decree. Thus when the letter from Jerusalem was shared with the daughter churches of Antioch in Galatia, Silas's presence undergirded the action. (2) He was a Roman citizen, as was Paul (16:37).

Barnabas and John Mark sailed once again to Cyprus, and Paul and Silas traveled through Syria and Cilicia, strengthening the churches along the way (15:40-41).

Circumcision of Timothy (16:1-5)

In the Lycaonian city of Lystra, Paul took special note of a certain disciple, whose name was Timothy (v. 1). The young man was esteemed highly by other believers in the area, and Paul decided that he wanted Timothy to join Silas and him on their mission (vv. 2-3). However, his mixed parentage posed a problem. His mother was a Jewess, but his father was a Greek. Since Timothy never had been circumcised, in the eyes of the Jews he was the uncircumcised son of a Greek father. Yet as the son of such a union, he was legally Jewish, and had been brought up in the Jewish faith (2 Tim. 3:15). For Timothy to remain uncircumcised would have created a needless hindrance to his witness in Jewish communities on the tour. In a sense the circumcision of Timothy legitimized him in Jewish eyes, for he was already a half-Jew. As a practical expedient, it removed a cause of prejudice against him and widened the range of his potential witness.

Paul's action in Timothy's circumcision is in sharp contrast to his insistence in Jerusalem that Titus not be circumcised (Gal. 2:1-5). However, the circumstances of the two cases were different. Titus was a Gentile, a trophy of the Gentile mission. The Judaizing faction in the Jerusalem church that insisted on Titus's circumcision taught that without it he could not be saved. They were identified with the same ultra-traditional emissaries in Antioch who had evoked a crisis by teaching that Gentile converts could not be saved apart from circumcision (15:1). To have yielded to the Judaizers' demands in either instance would have been a disastrous compromise of the gospel of God's grace.

Following Timothy's circumcision, the missionary team continued on its way through the Galatian cities where churches had been established on the first journey. Everywhere they visited they delivered the decrees decided on by the apostles and elders at the Jerusalem Council (v. 4). As a result, the churches were strengthened in the faith, and they were increasing in numbers daily (v. 5).

Call to Macedonia (16:6-15)

As they passed through the region of Phrygia and Galatia, they sought to enter the Roman province of Asia. However, the Holy Spirit forbade them to do so (v. 6). Later on the third missionary journey Paul would labor many months in Ephesus, the main city of Asia, but not now (19:1-41). Similarly when they tried to go northward into Bithynia, they were prohibited (v. 7). Thus they followed a course between these two destinations, and eventually reached Troas, a Mysian city. Here Paul had a vision at night in which a certain Macedonian man appeared saying, "Come over to Macedonia and help us" (v. 9).

Troas enjoyed an important place in the history of the region. The Trojan war had been fought near Troas. Xerxes, the ruler of Persia, had passed this way in his effort to conquer Greece. Julius Caesar had thought of moving his capital here after he had defeated Pompey in the battle of Pharsalia in 48-47 B.C.

Now Paul, an itinerant Jewish Christian missionary, had

come to Troas, a place made famous by the passage of so many of the world's great men. Yet in the larger perspective of history, one wonders whether or not what happened to Paul in Troas had a more lasting significance than all prior expeditions. Though the gospel may have reached Rome at an earlier date, as a result of Paul's obedience to the Macedonian call, other churches were planted in Europe.

Soon Paul and his companions boarded a ship in Troas bound for Macedonia. Harboring overnight at Samothrace, they reached the Macedonian port of Neapolis the next day (v. 11). From there, they traveled to Philippi, described as "a leading city" that enjoyed status as "a Roman colony" (v. 12). As a Roman colony, Philippi enjoyed certain rights of self-government, land ownership, and sometimes freedom from tribute and taxation. It was a little Rome away from home.

On the sabbath day, they went outside the gate to a riverside place where some women had gathered for prayer (v. 13). One of them was named Lydia, a business woman from Thyatira who was prosperous and was a devout worshiper of God. As Paul spoke, "the Lord opened her heart to respond to the things spoken by Paul" (v. 14). She and her household believed and were baptized, whereupon she invited Paul and his companions to be guests in her home (v. 15). Thus the church in Philippi was born on a river bank in a women's prayer meeting. As it grew and prospered, it became Paul's partner in spreading the gospel, providing financial support and encouragement again and again (Phil. 4:16). And one of Paul's choice letters in the New Testament was addressed to the church in Philippi.

You likely observed Luke's use of the first person pronouns ("we" and "us") in Acts 16:10-17. Others are found in Acts 20:5-16; 21:1-18; and 27:1—28:16. Acts 16:10-17 is the first of the so-called "we" passages in the Book of Acts. Some scholars tend to conclude from these passages that the author of Acts was one of Paul's companions at these junctures of his missionary work. Then with other considerations in mind, they infer that the author was Luke, the physician. Others may regard the "we" passages as a literary form adopted by an unknown author.

Imprisoned in Philippi (16:23-40)

Following the exorcism of a slave-girl whose fortune-telling brought a lot of money to her owners, Paul and Silas were taken before the chief magistrates in Philippi (vv. 16-19). They were charged with disturbing the peace and teaching customs that no law-abiding Roman could observe (vv. 20-21). Denying the accused due process of law, the magistrates ripped the clothes off Paul and Silas and ordered them flogged (v. 22). Then they threw them into prison, commanding the jailer to place them in maximum security (vv. 23-24).

But God often enables His servants to sing in strange places—places in which others may curse, despair, and even die. With wounds still hurting and with feet fastened in stocks, about midnight Paul and Silas began to pray and sing hymns of praise to God (v. 25).

In the miraculous aftermath, the Philippian jailer and his household were converted (vv. 26-34). Another barrier was overcome, as the gospel of God's grace reached a pagan, one who had no prior associations with the Jewish faith.

From Thessalonica to Athens
(17:1-34; Focal: 17:1-6,22-31)

Once the erring magistrates of Philippi learned that Paul and Silas were Roman citizens, whom they had abused, they nervously implored them to leave the city (16:35-39). Thus, after a brief visit with the brethren in Lydia's home (16:40), Paul and his missionary companions traveled through Amphipolis and Apollonia to Thessalonica (17:1).

Preaching in a Synagogue in Thessalonica (vv. 1-6)

Thessalonica was the chief city of Macedonia. Located on the Thermaic Gulf, it had the finest harbor in the province; thus its commercial importance was assured. Furthermore, the Via Ignatia, a Roman road that linked the Adriatic and Aegean Seas, passed through the city. Two Roman arches spanned this road. The one at the western entrance to the city was known as the Vardar Gate, taking its name from the River Vardar. An inscription found there, and confirmed by others in Thessalonica, identified local officials called "politarchs." This has archaeological significance, because prior to the discovery of these inscriptions the term was found only in Acts 17:6.[1]

Thessalonica enjoyed status as a free city, which meant that it had its own assembly and exercised considerable self-rule. Among its large population were Jews, who had been drawn to the city by its commercial advantages. Thus a synagogue was there, and as was Paul's custom, he attended its services. Indeed, Luke recorded that for three sabbaths in the synagogue, Paul reasoned with the worshipers from the Scriptures (v. 2). From the Bible, Paul provided evidence that the Messiah would fulfill His role through suffering and resurrection from the dead. Then he argued that these prophecies had their fulfillment in Jesus, "This Jesus whom I am proclaiming to you is the Christ" (v. 3).

The results of Paul's preaching in a Thessalonian synagogue were encouraging. Some Jews believed and joined Paul and Silas, as did the wives of several prominent citizens. But the greatest response came from the Gentile God-fearers, who were open to the gospel message.

When the Jews saw many of these God-fearing Gentiles following Paul and Silas, they became jealous and angry. After all, the Gentiles were the Jews' best prospects for proselytes to the Jewish faith. Thus, they recruited some of the city rabble from the marketplace to form a mob and go after Paul and Silas. Since they were being hosted in Jason's home, likely one of the Jewish converts, the mob sought them there (v. 5). However, neither one was present. Possibly Paul and Silas had been forewarned and had made good their escape. At any rate, the mob, thwarted in its effort to apprehend the missionaries, dragged Jason and some brethren before the city authorities (v. 6). They charged Jason with harboring men who were revolutionaries. The mob further charged that Paul and Silas had caused trouble in other places and they had come to Thessalonica, proclaiming Jesus as a rival to Caesar (v. 7).

The city authorities took such a charge seriously. Then they proceeded to take a pledge from Jason and the others (v. 9). The pledge was designed to prevent any further disturbance and likely demanded that Paul and Silas leave the city. The brethren immediately sent them away by night to Berea, about 50 miles away. Evidently Timothy rejoined them there.

In Berea, the missionaries repeated their strategy of going first to the synagogue. They were encouraged to find the Bereans unusually ready to search the Scriptures. Paul had made claims about the messianic hope set forth in the Old Testament and its fulfillment in Jesus. Now his hearers examined the Scriptures daily to determine whether or not these things were so (v. 11). The result was that many of the Jews believed, as did also a number of prominent Greek men and women (v. 12).

When news of Paul's preaching and the gospel success in Berea reached the Jewish community in Thessalonica, a number of them came to disrupt the work (v. 13). A similar hostility had been manifested in south Galatia on the first missionary journey, when Jews from Pisidian Antioch and Iconium pursued Paul and Barnabas to Lystra (14:19). Once again, Jewish animosity forced Paul to leave a city where the gospel had been planted with much promise. The brethren escorted him to Athens while Silas and Timothy remained in Macedonia (vv. 14-15). Later they would rejoin him in Achaia.

Paul's Message in Athens (vv. 22-31).

The glory days of Athens in the fifth and fourth centuries B.C. had long passed, but even in Paul's day the city remained the cultural center of Greece. Its university was world-renowned, and its prominent places were adorned with the workmanship of the great architects and sculptors of antiquity. Many of these works were temples, shrines, and images of pagan deities. Whereas today's visitors to Athens may look on these monuments as masterpieces of classical art, Paul looked on them with a characteristic Jewish loathing of all things idolatrous. To him, Athens was a "city full of idols," and his spirit was provoked within him, as he waited for Silas and Timothy to come from Macedonia (v. 16).

Taking advantage of the interval, Paul entered the synagogue and reasoned with the Jews and God-fearing Gentiles in attendance there. Also, he went to the marketplace daily and bore witness to any whom he could engage in conversation (v. 17). In doing so, he did not escape certain Epicurean and Stoic philosophers' attention. They rather scornfully wanted to learn more about his teaching, "What would this idle babbler wish to say?" (v. 18). The word translated **babbler** meant literally *seed-picker*, one who was like a bird picking up crumbs in a city street. They scornfully labeled Paul as one who had gathered scraps of learning at random and had dubious wares to peddle.

However, since the Athenians were renowned for their interest in hearing new things (v. 21), Paul was taken to the Areopagus so that he might explain his teaching (vv. 19-20). This was a court or council that among other responsibilities exercised authority in matters of religion and education. Likely, it had some control over public lecturers. In no sense was Paul's appearance before this body a judicial hearing, for he was not on trial. Rather he was asked to give an account of what seemed to his cultured hearers to be a strange philosophy.

There are several important features in Paul's message in the midst of the Areopagus.

A tactful beginning.—He began by observing that they were "very religious in all respects" (v. 22). To be sure, the word translated "religious" was capable of meaning "superstitious," but the council seemed to hear it as a compliment. One does not commend the gospel to those of a different culture by rudeness or insult.

A point of contact.—In his reference to the altar with the inscription, "TO AN UNKNOWN GOD," he found an appropriate place to begin his witness. He attempted to tell them about the God whose existence they acknowledged, but about whom they confessed their ignorance. This is a good example of situational or contextual witnessing.

A biblical witness without quoting Scripture.—At no point did Paul quote a passage from the Bible; yet, he bore witness to a thoroughly biblical understanding of God. He was the Creator of the world and all things in it. He was/is the Lord of heaven and earth; thus He did/does not live in temples made with hands (v. 24; see 1 Kings 8:27; Isa. 66:1-2; Acts 7:48-50). Also, "since He Himself gives to all life and breath and all things" (v. 25), He never stands in need of what His creatures could do for Him.

An affirmation of the unity of mankind.—Paul cut across the grain of Greek pride and prejudice by stating that God had made from one man (Adam) every nation on the face of the earth. Furthermore, He "determined their appointed times, and the boundaries of their habitation" (v. 26).

A statement of God's purpose.—God's intention in creating people was that everyone should seek Him, "though He is not far from each one of us" (v. 27; Ps. 145:18).

An appeal to Greek poets.—That God was the source of all life and things in the world and that He was in no way dependent on His creatures was understood by their own poets (v. 28). The line, "For we also are His offspring," was also quoted by the Cilician poet, Aratus (v. 28; the Stoic poet, Cleanthes, had a similar expression). Thus Paul argued, "Being then the offspring of God, we ought not to think that the Divine Nature is like gold or silver or stone, an image formed by the art and thought of man" (v. 29).

A Christian witness.—The God who had "overlooked the times of ignorance" has now called on people everywhere to repent (v. 30). He already has "fixed a day in which He will judge the world in righteousness through a Man whom He has appointed, having furnished proof to all men by raising Him from the dead" (v. 31).

At Paul's mention of the resurrection of the dead, some Athenians interrupted him with snide remarks. Some of them thought that such thoughts were repugnant. Others who were more restrained said that they would hear more from Paul later (v. 32). A few, however, believed, including Dionysius, who was a member of the Areopagus, and a woman named Damaris (v. 34).

Apparently, Paul founded no church in Athens. Yet it strains the evidence to say, as some have done, that Paul failed in Athens because he supposedly intellectualized the gospel. The people's failure to respond in faith to the gospel did not always denote the messenger's failure; it could be derived from the listeners' (hearers') failure.

Return to Antioch (18:18-23; Focal: 18:18-28)

From Athens, Paul went to Corinth, the capital of the province of Achaia and an important commercial center. There he met Aquila and Priscilla, who along with all other Jews had been banished from Rome by the Emperor Claudius. They shared the same trade as tentmakers (or leatherworkers) and Paul made his home with them (18:3). Every sabbath, he went to the synagogue and reasoned with the Jews and Greeks (18:4). But when Silas and Timothy arrived from Macedonia, Paul began to devote his full energies to the gospel, "solemnly testifying to the Jews that Jesus was the Christ" (18:5).[2] Eventually strong opposition, even blasphemy, forced Paul to leave the synagogue and to direct his efforts to the Gentiles (18:6). In the house of Titius Justus, a devout man who lived next door to the synagogue, Paul continued his ministry (18:7). Many Corinthians believed and were baptized, including Crispus, the leader of the synagogue, and his household (18:8). Reassured by the Lord in a vision that He had many people in the city, Paul remained there for eighteen months, teaching the word of God (18:9-11).

Even after the Jews had sought unsuccessfully to have him prosecuted before the judgment seat of the Roman proconsul Gallio, he stayed on (18:12-17). Finally, in company with Aquila and Priscilla, he set sail for Syria, having had his hair cut in Cenchrea because he was keeping a vow (v. 18). En route he stopped at Ephesus, where he entered the synagogue and sought to reason with the Jews (v. 19). They urged him to stay longer, but Paul refused, saying that he hoped God would permit him to return (v. 20).

Then leaving Aquila and Priscilla in Ephesus (v. 19), Paul continued his voyage, landing at Caesarea. From there he traveled to Antioch (v. 22). Nothing was disclosed regarding Paul's stay in Antioch. Indeed, verse 23 describes his arrival there and his departure on the third missionary journey. Once again, he passed through "the Galatian region and Phrygia, strengthening all the disciples" (v. 23).

The Ministry of Apollos (18:24-28)

In Ephesus, Priscilla and Aquila met an eloquent Alexandrian preacher named Apollos. He was mighty in the Scriptures (v. 24), and with great fervor "he was speaking and teaching accurately the things concerning Jesus" (v. 25). However, he did it as one who knew only the baptism preached by John the Baptist. Apparently he did not know baptism in the name of Jesus Christ such as Peter proclaimed at Pentecost (2:38).

When Priscilla and Aquila heard him, they recognized the deficiency in his understanding, and "they took him aside and explained to him the way of God more accurately" (v. 26). To Apollos' credit he was teachable and became a more adequate proclaimer of the gospel. Thus when he expressed the desire to go to Achaia, the Ephesian brethren encouraged him. They sent a letter commending him to the work there (v. 27). Their confidence was justified, because in Achaia "he powerfully refuted the Jews in public, demonstrating by the Scriptures that Jesus was the Christ" (v. 28).

Later Paul would acknowledge that Apollos "watered" the gospel seed, which God had enabled him to plant in Corinth (1 Cor. 3:6).

Lessons for Life from Acts 15:36—18:28

In witnessing across cultural barriers, there is a difference between flexibility and compromise.—To Paul, the circumcision of Timothy, whose mother was a Jewess, was a practical expedient rather than a compromise of the faith. Yet he felt that to circumcise Titus, a Gentile, would be a disastrous compromise (Gal. 2:3-5). Rigid people at both ends of the spectrum of grace have criticized him severely, for to them all flexibility is compromise. However, compromise does not know where to *stand*, and rigorism does not know where to *bend*. Actually cultural rigidity only serves to limit the range in which God can use our witness. A special problem arises when people tend to equate their rigidity with orthodoxy.

There is a when-ness, as well as a where-ness, to the Holy Spirit's leadership.—The same Holy Spirit who forbade Paul's preaching in Ephesus on the second missionary journey (16:7) directed him there on the third (19:1-41). *Time,* as well as *place,* must come under the superintendency of the sovereign Spirit of God.

Sometimes faith's finest tributes to God come in the darkest hours.—Beaten and with their feet in stocks in a Philippian jail for the sake of the gospel, Paul and Silas sang praises to God at midnight (16:25). The world does not understand this, for its joys are at the mercy of every whim and circumstance. However, the secret of joy rests in a right relationship with God and others (Phil. 4:10-13).

Thank God! for the Priscillas and Aquilas in churches.—When an inadequate understanding of the biblical message of salvation is found in one of our preachers, some know only the strategy of confrontation and dismissal. Priscilla and Aquila, the marvelous missionary couple, chose a more Christlike alternative. They took Apollos into their care and taught him "the way of God more accurately" (18:26). Thus God enabled them to have a vital role in developing one of His most effective witnesses.

---

1. See "Thessalonica," The Interpreter's Dictionary of the Bible Vol. IV (Nashville: Abingdon Press, 1962), 629.

2. Many believe that Paul wrote 1 and 2 Thessalonians after receiving the report of Silas and Timothy from Macedonia. Also, it may have been a gift from the Philippian church that relieved Paul of the necessity of earning his own livelihood at this time (Phil. 4:15-16).

Personal Learning Activities

---

1. According to Dr. MacGorman three features of Paul's missionary strategy are _____ , _____ , and _____ .
2. True _____ False _____ Paul wanted to take John Mark on the second journey, but Barnabas did not (15:36-38).
3. Two advantages of Paul's choosing Silas as a partner are (1) _____ (2) _____ (15:39-40).
4. _____, who joined Paul and Silas at Lystra, was circumcised because of the Jews (16:1-3).
5. As a result of the missionary team's delivering the message from the Jerusalem Council the churches were (1) _____ _____ and (2) _____ (16:4-5).

6. After being prevented by _____ from going into the province of Asia or turning north, Paul received a _____ to go west into _____ (16:6-9).
7. Philippi was a _____ colony (16:12).
8. _____ was the first convert at Philippi (16:13-15).
9. Underline the correct answer. In Philippi, God used Paul to (1) reach a lady and her household, (2) heal a girl of demon possession, (3) save a jailer and family, (4) all three.
10. What means of witnessing did Paul and Silas use in the prison in Philippi? _____ and _____ _____ .
11. True _____ False _____ Paul proved from the Scriptures that Jesus was the Messiah (17:1-3).
12. In Thessalonica so many people _____ that the Jews got jealous and persecuted them (17:1-10).
13. The Bereans were commended for their unusual willingness to _____ _____ _____ (17:11-12).
14. True _____ False _____ Paul communicated the gospel in Athens by referring to their religious bent, quoting their poets, then presenting a Christian witness (17:22-31).
15. Aquila and Priscilla demonstrated the following characteristics: (1) believers, (2) tentmakers, (3) had been to Rome, (4) met Paul in Corinth and accompanied him to Ephesus, (5) instructed Apollos, (6) all of the above.
16. True _____ False _____ Apollos would have made a wonderful Christian, but he never would accept Jesus as Lord.

7

Paul's Continued Missionary Work

Acts 19:1—21:14

The Book of Acts records Paul's three missionary journeys. Already we have studied two of them, as they were recorded in Acts 13:1—14:28 and in 15:36—18:22. In chapter six, we even probed the beginning of the third journey (18:23-28). Now, we will resume our study of Paul's third and final recorded journey, noting his efforts to spread the gospel into new areas as well as to strengthen existing churches.

Some interesting comparisons can be made regarding these three journeys:

1. *Background.*—The first one took place in the context of the dramatic meeting in Antioch, in which the Holy Spirit called Barnabas and Paul to launch the Gentile mission (13:1-3). The second one followed on the crucial meeting of the Jerusalem Council (15:1-35). But no such momentous events formed the background for the third journey. Indeed, the same verse (18:23) describes both the end of the second journey and the beginning of the third. No clear break separates them.

2. *Companions.*—Barnabas and John Mark accompanied Paul on the first journey. Silas, and later Timothy, accompanied him on the second. Luke did not identify any companion as Paul began the third journey.

3. *Primary location.*—The first tour focused primarily on preaching the gospel and establishing churches in south Galatia. On the second journey, Paul spent more time in Corinth than in any other city, and on the third he spent about three years in Ephesus. In all, he invested approximately five years of his missionary labors establishing churches in these two great port cities on the western and eastern shores of the-

Aegean Sea.

4. *Return to Antioch.*—At the end of both the first and second journeys, Paul returned to Antioch of Syria as the home base for his mission to the Gentiles. However, his arrest in Jerusalem and imprisonment in Caesarea at the conclusion of his third journey prevented him from returning to Antioch.

5. *Future plans.*—In Acts 19:21, Paul stated his intention to go to Rome after completing his visits to Macedonia, Achaia, and Jerusalem. Evidently he felt that his work in the eastern Mediterranean areas was drawing to a close (Rom. 15:23). And from Romans 15:24,28, we learn that Paul wanted the church at Rome to become the missionary base for his intended evangelization of Spain.

The focal passages of this chapter will include the following features of Paul's third missionary journey: his ministry in Ephesus (19:1-6,20-23); his travel through Macedonia and Achaia (20:1-3); his visit with the Ephesian elders at Miletus (20:17-30); and his stay with Philip in Caesarea, en route to Jerusalem (21:7-14).

Ministry in Ephesus (19:1-6,20-23)

In Paul's day, Ephesus was a large ancient city—the capital of the Roman province of Asia and, indeed, a great commercial center for all Asia Minor. It had a fine harbor at the mouth of the Cayster River, though continuous dredging was required to keep it from silting up. Today the ruins of the ancient city lie four or five miles inland from the sea.

The location of Ephesus on the main route from Rome to the eastern Mediterranean enhanced its commercial importance. Also, the city enjoyed political significance as the capital of the Roman province of Asia. Its status as a free city included the right to its own civic assembly and considerable self-rule.

Ephesians were particularly proud of their city's acclaim as the "guardian of the temple of the great Artemis" (v. 35). For Artemis was a cult goddess, whose temple in Ephesus was justly renowned as one of the seven wonders of the ancient world. Indeed, many citizens derived lucrative incomes from crafts and trades related to her worship.

Disciples of John the Baptist (vv. 1-6)

After Apollos left to minister in Corinth, Paul went to Ephesus, where he found some disciples (v. 1). He asked them if they had received the Holy Spirit when they believed. Behind this question was the tacit assumption that this was usually when believers received the Holy Spirit. When the gospel was proclaimed, the Holy Spirit convicted hearers of their sins and of Jesus Christ's adequacy to save. The new converts made public their profession of faith by submitting to baptism. At this time, the Holy Spirit usually took up residence in the heart of believers. We have noted some variations in this pattern in Samaria, where the Holy Spirit was received after baptism (8:14-17), and in Caesarea, where the Holy Spirit was received before baptism (10:44-48). However, Paul's question assumed that converts received the Holy Spirit at the time of baptism. To his question Paul received the startling answer "No, we have not even heard whether there is a Holy Spirit" (v. 2). Then when he asked the Ephesian disciples into what they had been baptized, they replied, "Into John's baptism" (v. 3).

Immediately one wonders how these disciples could have been baptized into John's baptism without ever hearing that there was a Holy Spirit. Mark 1:8 records John the Baptist's preaching regarding the Coming One, "I baptized you with water; but He will baptize you with the Holy Spirit." (See also the parallel passages in Matt. 3:11 and Luke 3:16.) Surely, if they ever had heard John preach, or if his preaching had been reported to them adequately, they would have heard about the Holy Spirit.

Devout scholars have proposed a variety of solutions to this problem. For example, F. F. Bruce suggested that these Ephesian believers knew that John had spoken of the coming baptism with the Holy Spirit. However, they did not know that it was an accomplished fact. Theirs was "the pre-Pentecostal" baptism as proclaimed and administered by John the Baptist—a baptism of expectation rather than one of fulfillment, as Christian baptism now was."[1] Similarly Frank Stagg stated, "It was not necessarily the Holy Spirit's existence, but his presence, that was unknown to them."[2] Taking note of the preceding passage about Apollos (18:24-28), others have speculated that these men may have regarded themselves as followers of John the Baptist and Apollos. Or were they members of a John the Baptist sect in Ephesus?

The passage is admittedly obscure, and we will have to settle for less than we would like to know about these disciples. However, that they did not even understand John's baptism is obvious, for Paul had to show them that it was a preparation for the coming of Jesus (v. 4). Having been instructed, these men who had been baptized into John's baptism, were rebaptized in the name of the Lord Jesus (v. 5). This is the only instance of rebaptism in the New Testament. Then when Paul laid his hands on them, "the Holy Spirit came on them, and they began speaking with tongues and prophesying" (v. 6).

There is no fixed pattern in the Book of Acts regarding baptism, the laying on of hands, the receiving of the Holy Spirit, and the external manifestations of the Spirit. As noted earlier in the study of Acts 2:37-42; 8:14-17; and 10:44-48, there may or may not be the laying on of hands. Also, there may or may not be external manifestations of the Spirit. However, all who believed in Jesus Christ as Lord and Savior submitted to baptism, and all who were baptized received the Holy Spirit, whether simultaneous with, after, or before baptism.

Success of the Word in Asia (vv. 20-23)

Following the apostle's encounter with John's disciples, Luke described Paul's continued ministry in Ephesus. For three months, he spoke out boldly about the kingdom of God in the synagogue (v. 8). However, as earlier in Corinth (18:6-7), he eventually encountered such opposition that he was forced to leave. He resumed his gospel labors in the school of Tyrannus, where he continued for two years (v. 9). With Ephesus as a base, the gospel spread to surrounding areas, as Paul's co-workers planted churches in cities such as Colossae, Hierapolis, and Laodicea. In fact, Luke stated that during this time all who lived in the Roman province of Asia, Jews and Greeks alike, heard the word of the Lord (v. 10). And we know that the province remained a leading center of Christian witness for several centuries.

In this center of magic, pagan superstition, and idolatry, God performed extraordinary miracles through Paul, especially those of healing and exorcism (vv. 11-12). But when the seven sons of Sceva, described as a Jewish chief priest, tried to exorcise in Jesus' name, they were routed by the demonic spirit (vv. 15-16). Sceva was not an official high priest of the Temple in Jerusalem, for we know the names of the high priests of this period, and he was not one of them. Likely he was self-designated as high priest, an impostor.

Word of the incident spread rapidly, and it had a dramatic effect on all who heard it. Jesus' name was magnified (v. 17), and believers, who still held to their magic charms and spells, finally broke with them (v. 18). Practitioners of magic brought their magical papyri and parchments, worth a large sum of money, to be burned (v. 19). Thus the Lord's word was growing mightily and prevailing throughout the entire region (v. 20).

At this point in Luke's narrative, he inserted a note about Paul's future travel plans. He intended to go to Jerusalem by way of Macedonia and Achaia. Then he expressed the desire to see Rome (v. 21). In preparation for his visit, Paul sent two of his co-workers, Timothy and Erastus, on ahead to Macedonia, while he remained in Asia a while longer (v. 22).

However, as the gospel succeeded throughout the province, the hostility of the silversmiths and related craftsmen, whose livelihood was derived from the worship of Artemis, mounted. There had been a falling off in the demand for their wares, and they felt threatened by the loss of income. By linking the declining profits to the loss of esteem for Artemis, Demetrius, a silversmith, was able to stir up a riot (vv. 24-28). The angry mob dragged two of Paul's Macedonian companions, Gaius and Aristarchus, into the great theater of Ephesus (v. 29). But when Paul sought to enter, his friends, both Christians and pagan officials, persuaded him not to do so (vv. 30-32).

Eventually, the town clerk brought order out of the confusion. He was the secretary of the city council and the convener of the assembly, the most important native official in Ephesus. He acted as the liaison officer between the local government and the Roman provincial administration, headquartered in Ephesus. He assured his unruly hearers that everyone acknowledged that Ephesus was the guardian of the temple of Artemis (vv. 35-36). He urged that Demetrius and his fellow-craftsmen press whatever charges they had against Paul and his companions in the courts, or, if necessary, in the assembly (vv. 37-39). He warned that their riotous action had placed the favored status of their city in jeopardy (v. 40). For Rome had a remarkably low tolerance for riots or insurrection.

Ministry in Macedonia and Achaia (20:1-38; Focal: 20:1-3,17-30)

Not long after the Ephesian uproar, Paul gathered the disciples for final instructions and encouragement, and then left for Macedonia (v. 1). At this point, Luke gave an exceedingly brief account of Paul's missionary activities. In just two verses, he covered several months of Paul's work in Macedonia and Achaia; the Jewish plot against Paul's life as he prepared to set sail for Syria; and his changed travel plans (vv. 2-3). He determined to return by land through Macedonia, in order to foil the murderous intent of his enemies.

Verse 4 names several of Paul's traveling companions from the Gentile churches, who went on ahead of him to Troas (v. 5). Actually, the churches had chosen them to accompany Paul to Jerusalem with a relief offering for needy believers there. By this expression of sacrificial love, Paul hoped not only to alleviate physical hardship but also to help heal the breach between Jewish and Gentile Christians.

In the second "we" passage of Acts (20:5-16), Luke described the voyage from Philippi to Miletus, with stops of varying lengths at Troas (vv. 7-12), Assos (v. 13), Mitylene (v. 14), and presumably Samos (v. 15). Paul had decided to bypass Ephesus, because he was hurrying to reach Jerusalem in time for Pentecost (v. 16).

Meeting with the Ephesian Elders at Miletus (20:17-30)

Miletus was about thirty miles from Ephesus. While the ship was docked there, Paul sent a request to the Ephesian church elders to come for a meeting with him. They came, and in verses 17-30, Paul delivered his only speech to Christians that was recorded in the Book of Acts. With ominous forebodings of what awaited him in Jerusalem, he gave them his farewell message before his ship put out to sea. Several features of his message merit our attention.

Remembrance and Personal Defense (vv. 18-21)

Certain parts of the larger passage sound as though Paul were defending himself against criticism. One wonders if some had begun to find fault with him while he was ministering in Macedonia and Achaia. Later in his message, he warned against those in the congregation who would seek to draw away disciples after themselves (v. 30). Preliminary to such a devious tactic, some usually seek to undermine others' confidence in existing leaders. At any rate, Paul reminded the elders of his past ministry in their midst. It had been rendered under tense and trying circumstances due to the Jews' plots (v. 19). Yet he did not shrink from declaring to them anything that was profitable. This was done publicly, as in the daily sessions in the school of Tyrannus (19:8), and from house-to-house (v. 20). He had one message for both Jews and Gentiles, namely, "repentance toward God and faith in our Lord Jesus Christ" (v. 21). (Compare with Mark's summation of Jesus' preaching, Mark 1:14-15.)

Repentance meant *a changing of mind and direction.* It demanded that one renounce old life-patterns, in which sin and self were enthroned and God was ignored, rebelled against, or denied. Repentance has been inherent in the call to faith, for no one can turn to God without turning from sin. And faith never can be a detached assent that certain truths about Jesus Christ are true. Faith is trusting in and commitment to the Lord. Faith also includes loving obedience to His will. Thus Paul's past ministry among the Ephesians was characterized by a difficult context, a diligent service, and a faithful message.

Impending Plans (vv. 22-27)

Paul was under a divine compulsion to go to Jerusalem, though he was not sure of what would happen to him there (v. 22). On an earlier occasion, following his return to the city after his conversion on the road to Damascus, Hellenistic Jews had tried to put him to death (9:29). On his present trip to Jerusalem, he had been forced to change his travel plans in Achaia to escape the Jews' murderous plot (20:3). Furthermore, in every city on his return itinerary the Holy Spirit had borne solemn testimony that bonds and afflictions awaited him in Jerusalem (v. 23). Indeed, in Romans 15:31, written shortly before his departure from Achaia, he had requested prayer for deliverance from those in Judea who were disobedient to the gospel.

Fully aware that to return to Jerusalem could cost him his life, he placed priority on finishing his course in the gospel ministry (v. 24; see 2 Tim. 4:7). He did not count his life as dear to himself, but wanted above all else to fulfill the calling he had received from the Lord Jesus (see Phil. 1:20). He felt certain that his Ephesian brethren never would see his face again (v. 25). And it meant much to him that his faithful declaration of "the whole purpose of God" had rendered him innocent of the blood of all men (vv. 26-27; compare Ezek. 33:1-9).

Warning against Enemies (vv. 28-30)

A part of declaring to Paul's hearers the full counsel of God was to warn them against impending dangers. They were the overseers of the flock, so-called and equipped by the Holy Spirit to serve. They had the responsibility "to shepherd the church of God which He purchased with His own blood" (v. 28). Paul warned that after his departure, men described as "savage wolves" would come in from the outside and would not spare the flock (v. 29). Other enemies would arise from within the church, speaking perverse things and seeking to build up a following for themselves (v. 30). How necessary then that the leaders of the church remain on the alert!

In such counsel, Paul was asking of the Ephesian elders what he himself had demonstrated in their midst (v. 31). Then he commended them to the grace of God (v. 32), and reminded them that he never had coveted anyone's wealth or wardrobe (v. 33). Among them, he had earned his own livelihood and in addition had sought to provide help for others (v. 34). Hard work, charitable concern, and glad remembrance of the Lord's instructions at this point constituted his order of the day. For Jesus had taught His followers, " 'It is more blessed to give than to receive' " (v. 35).

One will look in vain to find this saying of Jesus in the Gospels, though there are sayings that reveal a similar spirit; for example, Luke 6:38; 11:9-13. Possibly this saying appeared in a collection of Jesus' sayings in circulation during Paul's time. Or it may have been passed on orally from one to another.

Paul concluded his meeting with the church leaders from Ephesus with prayer (v. 36). Grieving over the prospects of never seeing him again, the elders wept aloud as they embraced and kissed him repeatedly (v. 37). Sorrowfully, they accompanied him to the ship (v. 38).

Acts 21:1-6 describes the voyage from Miletus to Tyre on the Phoenician coast. While the ship's cargo was being unloaded, Paul and his companions enjoyed a week's fellowship with the disciples who lived there (vv. 3-4). Even in Tyre, Paul received repeated warnings not to set foot in Jerusalem, but he would not be dissuaded. Finally the families of believers escorted the travelers to the beach for final prayers and farewells, as Paul resolutely continued on his journey (vv. 5-6).

With Philip the Evangelist in Caesarea (21:7-14; Focal: 21:7-14)

From Tyre, Paul and his party sailed to Ptolemais, about 25 miles distant. There they greeted the brethren and remained with them for a day (v. 7). The following day they arrived at Caesarea, and were accommodated in the home of Philip the evangelist, described as "one of the seven" (v. 8; 6:3,5).

Luke recorded that Philip had four virgin daughters who were prophetesses (v. 9). Presumably this meant that the sovereign Spirit of God had endowed them with the gift of prophecy. When exercised, they prophesied or spoke God's message to their hearers. This was an instance of the fulfillment of Joel's prophecy, which Peter cited in his great message on the day of Pentecost (2:17-18).

During Paul's stay in Caesarea, a prophet named Agabus gave Paul a dramatic warning. Likely, this was the same prophet who earlier came to Antioch and prophesied about a coming famine (11:28). But in this instance, he took Paul's belt and bound his own hands and feet. Then he declared by the authority of the Holy Spirit that in Jerusalem the Jews would so bind Paul and deliver him to the Gentiles (v. 11).

Agabus' spectacular demonstration prompted Paul's associates and the local residents to plead fervently that he not go to Jerusalem (v. 12). Paul was moved by their impassioned concern for his welfare, but declared his willingness to die, if necessary, in Jerusalem for the name of the Lord Jesus (v. 13).

Seeing that no amount of persuasion could deter Paul from his course, they finally ceased their efforts, saying, "The will of the Lord be done!" (v. 14).

Lessons for Life from Acts 19:1—21:14

People do not part easily with old superstitions.—Not until the dramatic routing of the seven sons of Sceva did some of the Ephesian believers part with their good luck charms and spells. Perhaps today, some believers still read their Bible and check their horoscopes in a local newspaper on the same day.

There is a temptation to shrink from the declaration of the whole counsel of God.—My Baptist preacher father one time described the joy and anticipation of standing in the pulpit when the Lord had given him a message of gospel hope for the people. By the same token, he described the dread of preaching when the same Lord had laid a message of judgment on his heart. Furthermore, most congregations prefer a message on love to one on judgment, though the same Spirit of God inspired both messages. We need to remember that in times of faithlessness and danger, admonition is love's authentic expression.

The call to repentance is inseparable from the call to faith.—The gospel preached by Jesus declared, " 'The time is fulfilled, and the kingdom of God is at hand; repent and believe the gospel' " (Mark 1:15). As the call to repentance was inseparable from the call to faith in Jesus' preaching, so it must be in ours. Does it seem to you that in recent years the call to repent has become a muted note on the gospel trumpet? If so, we need to remember that we never can improve on Jesus' preaching.

Each believer is responsible for discerning and following the Spirit of God's leadership.—Had the decision regarding Paul's trip to Jerusalem been determined by a majority vote, his friends, and eventually his closest associates, would have kept him from going. However, God reserves to Himself the ultimate part for each of His children's walk with Him. None must intervene in this privacy, even when Spirit-prompted discernment becomes aware of the dangers ahead.

---

1. F. F. Bruce, *The Book of the Acts* (Grand Rapids, MI: Wm. B. Eerdmans Pub. Co., 1973), 386.
2. Frank Stagg, *The Book of Acts* (Nashville: Broadman Press, 1955), 197.

Personal Learning Activities

1. Paul invested almost four years of ministry in what two port cities on the Aegean Sea? (18:1,11; 19:1,10) _____ and _____ .

2. Paul's main message to the Jews in Corinth was that " _____ _____ _____ _____ " (18:5)

3. True _____ False _____ The only instance of rebaptism recorded in the New Testament is when some followers of

John were baptized in the name of Jesus (19:5).

4. Although the pattern varied, all who believed in Jesus as Savior submitted to _____ and all who were baptized received _____ _____ _____ (19:5-6).

5. True _____ False _____ When those who practiced magic in Ephesus accepted Jesus as Lord, they confessed their sins and burned the books of magic publicly (19:18-19).

6. _____ was a cult goddess whose temple in Ephesus was one of the seven wonders of the ancient world (19:24).

7. From a strong base in _____ the gospel spread throughout the province of Asia (19:26).

8. The only speech made specifically to Christians in Acts is Paul's message to the _____ _____ _____ (20:17-38).

9. The message which Paul proclaimed publicly and from house-to-house to Jews and Gentiles was _____ toward God and _____ in our Lord Jesus Christ (20:21).

10. Why did Paul feel he was "innocent of the blood of all men" (20:26-27)? _____

_____ .

11. True _____ False _____ Paul received much encouragement to return to Jerusalem (21:1-14).

12. Philip's four daughters were _____ (21:9).

13. Through a dramatic demonstration, the prophet _____ indicated that Paul would be bound if he went to Jerusalem. When Paul would not be dissuaded, the people said: "_____ _____ _____ ___ ___ _____ ___ " (21:10-14).

14. What experience have you had that proves that each believer is responsible for discerning and following the Spirit of God's leadership. _____

_____

_____

8

On Trial for the Faith
Acts 21:15—26:32

The Lord's words regarding Paul to Ananias in Damascus have a climactic fulfillment in the overall passage for this chapter. At that time, Paul the persecutor was languishing in the house of Judas, blinded from his encounter with the risen Lord on the way into the city (9:11-12). The Lord instructed Ananias, "Go, for he is a chosen instrument of Mine, to bear My name before the Gentiles and kings and the sons of Israel; for I will show him how much he must suffer for My name's sake" (9:15-16).

Several years of gospel ministry had passed, and Paul had returned to Jerusalem for the last time. He was strangely compelled by the Holy Spirit to do so in the face of danger. Within a few days of his arrival, he was attacked by an angry Jewish mob. Apart from the Roman soldiers' intervention, he would have been assassinated in the temple area (21:27-36).

In the aftermath of the Jews' attempt on his life, Paul bore a faithful testimony to the "brethren and fathers"(22:1). Paul bore his witness when the Roman commander permitted him to address the enraged Jews from the steps leading to the barracks (21:37—22:21). This was true also on the day after the riot, when he made his defense before the Jewish council (22:30—23:10).

To thwart a Jewish plot to ambush Paul, the Roman commander transferred him under military escort to Caesarea, the seat of Roman administration in Judea (23:12-35). In the trials that followed before Felix and Festus, who served successively as governors in the province, Paul bore the Lord's name before the Gentiles also (24:1—25:12).

Then when King Agrippa and his sister Bernice came to Caesarea to pay their respects to Festus, the new governor,

Paul bore a Christian testimony before the last of the Herodian kings (25:13—26:32).

All of these things Paul endured for the sake of the Lord's name. The following discussion will highlight Paul's faithfulness under trial.

Falsely Accused in Jerusalem
(21:27-28; Focal: 21:27-28)

Paul's return to Jerusalem was greeted by the church with both gladness and apprehension. Surely the Gentile churches' relief offering which they sent to alleviate the Jewish Christians' hardship must have brought some joy. Yet Luke was surprisingly silent about this major project of the third missionary journey. As Paul narrated God's accomplishments among the Gentiles, the church glorified God (vv. 19-20). However, James and the elders were concerned about the Jewish believers' possible reaction to Paul's presence in the city. False reports had been circulated among them to the effect that Paul had been teaching the Jews of the Dispersion to forsake Moses, "telling them not to circumcise their children nor to walk according to the customs" (v. 21).

To repudiate the rumors and to forestall possible trouble, the Jerusalem leaders urged Paul to sponsor four men who were under a vow, purifying himself along with them (v. 24). Though the vow was not identified, it was likely a temporary Nazirite vow, in which the worshiper separated himself in a special way to the Lord (Num. 6:1-21). Neither did Luke give the reason for Paul's rite of purification. Some scholars have proposed that it was to take care of the ceremonial defilement that Paul had incurred through living among the Gentiles. Others have suggested that the four had contracted a ritual defilement accidentally while taking their Nazirite vows and that Paul was to pay their expenses and undergo purification with them.

However well intended, the plan miscarried when certain Jews from Asia saw Paul in the temple and cried out their false accusations against him. They charged him with preaching against his own people, the law, and the temple. (Compare with the charges against Stephen in 6:11-14.) Also, they claimed that he had defiled the temple by bringing Greeks into it. The last charge was particularly dangerous, for any non-Jew who ventured into the temple beyond the Court of the Gentiles was liable to the death penalty.[1] Of course, none of Paul's accusers actually had seen him take a Gentile into the temple. Rather they had seen Trophimus, an Ephesian believer, with Paul in the city, and they supposed that Paul had taken him into the temple (v. 29). Sometimes people who are blinded by religious hatred do not feel any necessity to verify their accusations against others. And unfortunately, they seem to find mobilizing a noisy and violent rabble to further their ends easy.

Thus the infuriated Jews rushed on Paul in the temple, dragged him outside, and were trying to kill him (vv. 30-31). However, the Roman commander and his soldiers intervened and rescued Paul (v. 32). Unable to learn anything about his identity and the grievance against him because of the uproar, the commander ordered that Paul be taken into the barracks (vv. 33-34). When Paul spoke to him in Greek, the commander asked whether or not he were the Egyptian leader who had escaped after leading a revolt of the assassins (v. 38). Paul replied that he was a Jew of Tarsus in Cilicia and asked permission to address the mob that had tried to kill him (vv. 39-40).

Addressing Enraged Jews
(22:1-21; Focal: 22:1-21)

When the Roman commander granted Paul's request, he began to address the enraged Jews from the stairs which led from the outer court of the temple into the barracks (the tower of Antonia). He spoke in the Hebrew dialect or Aramaic, and this had a quieting effect on his hearers (v. 2). What followed was both a personal defense and a testimony.

His Former Zeal in Judaism (vv. 3-6)
Paul identified himself as a Jew of the Dispersion, having been born in Tarsus of Cilicia. However, he was reared in Jerusalem, and educated strictly according to the law of the fathers under the instruction of the renowned Gamaliel (v. 3).

As for the followers of the Way, Paul had regarded them as

renegades to the true faith of Israel. Thus he had felt that he was doing God's will by persecuting them, putting both men and women into prisons (v. 4; Gal. 1:13-14). So intense was his hostility toward the Christians that he sought and received from the high priest and council the authority to return to Jerusalem those who had fled to Damascus for refuge (v. 5). Indeed, he had made his way along the road to Damascus as a prosecutor and persecutor of Christians.

Paul's Conversion on the Way to Damascus (vv. 6-16)

As Paul approached the city about noontime, he said that a bright heavenly light suddenly flashed all around him (v. 6). Overwhelmed, he fell to the ground and heard a voice saying,

"Saul, Saul, why are you persecuting Me?" (v. 7). And when he asked for the identity of the voice, the risen Lord replied, "I am Jesus the Nazarene, whom you are persecuting" (v. 8). Others in Paul's traveling party saw the dazzling light, but did not understand the voice of the One who was speaking to him (v. 9).

When Paul asked what he was supposed to do, he was told to continue his journey into Damascus, where he would receive further instruction (v. 10). Blinded by the brightness of the heavenly light, he had to be led by the hand into the city (v. 11). There a man named Ananias came and ministered to him. Since Paul was addressing a crowd of angry Jews, he emphasized that Ananias was "devout by the standard of the Law, and well spoken of by all the Jews who lived there" (v. 12).

Through Ananias' faithful ministry, God restored Paul's sight (v. 13). Also, Ananias explained, "The God of our fathers has appointed you to know His will, and to see the Righteous One, and to hear an utterance from His mouth. For you will be a witness for Him to all men of what you have seen and heard" (vv. 14-15). On the basis of this divine revelation and call (See also Gal. 1:15-16), Ananias urged Paul, "Arise, and be baptized, and wash away your sins, calling on His name" (v. 16).

His Warning and Commission (vv. 17-21)

Paul moved from the account of his conversion in Damascus, to a description of a dramatic event that took place when he returned to Jerusalem. He was in the temple praying, when he fell into a trance and saw the Lord, who warned him to leave the city immediately. The reason for this admonition was that the Jews would not accept his testimony about the Lord (v. 18).

Paul found this explanation hard to accept. He felt that his past history as a persecutor of Christians should predispose the Jews to give him a hearing. They knew that previously he had gone from one synagogue to another imprisoning and beating believers (v. 19). They knew that he had approved when others had stoned Stephen and he had guarded their cloaks while they slew him (v. 20). With this background experience, would not the Jerusalem Jews be all the more eager to hear about the dramatic change in his life?

Paul's line of thought was not unreasonable. For Paul, Jesus

Christ had brought a total reversal to his life which constituted undeniable evidence of the truth of the gospel that he preached. Those who had known him best in his former years as a persecutor of Christians should have been the first to want to hear him testify to how Jesus Christ had changed his life. Indeed, this was true of the Judean Christians who heard about his conversion, for they stood on common ground (Gal. 1:22-24). However, that was not true of the angry Jews who stood before Paul in the outer court of the temple. They looked on him as he formerly had looked on Jesus' followers. And in their efforts to kill him, they tried to do what Paul had done previously and for the same reason.

Thus the Lord had said to Paul during his vision in the temple, "Go! For I will send you far away to the Gentiles" (v. 21).

Up to this point, the Jews had been listening to Paul. But with the statement about his commission to preach the gospel to the Gentiles, their simmering rage boiled over in a noisy demonstration. They cried out for his death, "throwing off their cloaks and tossing dust into the air" (v. 23). The commander issued an order for Paul to be taken into the barracks, where he intended to learn the reason for the uproar by having Paul examined by scourging (v. 24). To avoid this excruciating and needless procedure, Paul appealed to his rights as a Roman citizen (v. 25). When this knowledge was conveyed to the commander, he became apprehensive and asked Paul if it were so (vv. 26-27). His own citizenship had cost a large sum of money. Paul replied, "But I was actually born a citizen" (v. 28). Thus Paul escaped the scourging but he was held in custody (v. 29).

Reassurance from the Lord (23:11; Focal: 23:11)

On the day following the riot in the temple, the Roman commander ordered the Jewish council to assemble in an effort to determine their grievance against Paul (22:30). Placed before his accusers, Paul began his defense by claiming a clear conscience before God (23:1). Whereupon the chief priest Ananias commanded those standing nearby to strike him on the mouth (23:2). Stung both by the blow and its injustice, Paul rebuked the chief priest for violating the law while presumably adjudicating it (23:3). In turn, he was rebuked for reviling the high priest, and apparently accepted the correction (23:4-5).

Paul's statement that he did not realize he was addressing the high priest has prompted several explanations: (1) This was not a regular session of the Sanhedrin, but a meeting convened and presided over by the military tribune. (2) Paul's visits to Jerusalem for the past several years had been sporadic and brief; thus he actually did not know the high priest personally. (3) Paul spoke sarcastically, saying in effect, "Who would expect the high priest to make such a mockery of his office!"

With this abusive interruption, Paul changed his approach. He claimed that he was being tried for nurturing the hope of the resurrection (23:6). Immediately this claim caused a heated dissension between the Sadducees and Pharisees who were in the assembly (23:7). The Sadducees believed neither in the resurrection nor angels and spirits; whereas the Pharisees did (23:8). Thus the Pharisees began to moderate in their attitude toward Paul, allowing that perhaps an angel or a spirit had spoken to him (23:9). But to the Sadducees this was nonsense, and with their accusations against Paul now confused with their theological differences, the Roman commander had to intervene again. Fearing that Paul would be torn to pieces by them, he took him by force and returned him to the safety of the barracks (23:10).

That night the Lord stood at Paul's side to reassure him, saying, "Take courage; for as you have solemnly witnessed to My cause at Jerusalem, so you must witness at Rome also" (23:11).

Paul's experience was similar to an earlier crisis in Corinth. There in a nighttime vision, the Lord assured Paul of safety and success in hostile surroundings (18:9-10).

Imprisoned in Caesarea
(24:24-27; Focal: 24:24-27)

So intent were the Jews on killing Paul that over 40 of them took an oath neither to eat nor drink until they had accomplished his death (23:12-14). They planned to have the council request a further hearing of Paul. Then while he was being brought to the meeting place, they would ambush him (23:15).

However, Paul's nephew learned about the plot, and told him about it (23:16). Whereupon Paul had a centurion take his nephew to the commander with this information (23:17-22). Learning about it, the commander determined to protect his accused but untried prisoner. So under military escort, he sent him to the governor, Felix, in Caesarea (23:23-24). A letter detailing the case was sent along, and from its salutation we learn that the commander's name was Claudius Lysias (23:26-30). On his arrival in Caesarea, Paul was kept under custody in Herod's Praetorium, the governor's official residence (23:31-35).

Five days later the high priest Ananias, some elders, and an attorney named Tertullus came to Caesarea to press their charges against Paul in the provincial court (24:1-2). Paul was maligned as a troublemaker among the Jews everywhere and "a ringleader of the sect of the Nazarenes" (24:5). Also, the same false charge of desecrating the temple that incited the riot in Jerusalem was reiterated in Caesarea (24:6). Evidently the Jewish religious leaders made no effort to verify the charge.

Tertullus' statement "we arrested him" implied an orderly procedure, obscuring the fact that a Jewish mob had sought to kill Paul (24:6). Also, his report that Lysias "with much violence took him out of our hands" faulted the manner in which the commander had intruded upon their alleged orderly judicial process (24:7). Actually, he ordered his soldiers to intervene at a time when he feared that Paul would be torn to pieces by them (20:30-32). But religious leaders who were cast in the mold of an Ananias were capable of perjury without a twinge of conscience.

In response to the charges, Paul denied all wrong. None of his accusers could prove that he was guilty of inciting a riot, and the brevity of the time since his arrival in Jerusalem scarcely allowed the claim (24:11-13). He acknowledged that he was a follower of the Way, "believing everything that is in accordance with the Law, and that is written in the Prophets" (24:14). Also, he affirmed his belief in "a resurrection of both the righteous and the wicked" (24:15). His reasons for going up to Jerusalem were to worship God (24:11) and to bring alms to his people and to present offerings (24:17). His accusers in the temple were "certain Jews from Asia," whose absence from the courtroom in Caesarea denied him the right of facing them (24:18-19). And his present accusers in the provincial court could not indict him for any misdeed. However, he did shout in the midst of their deliberations that he was on trial for his belief in the resurrection of the dead (24:20-21).

After hearing the Jews' charges and Paul's defense, Felix determined to delay his judgment until he could hear Lysias's testimony. In the meantime, Paul would be kept in custody with some freedom and the services of his friends (24:22-23).

These events provided the background for Paul's meeting with Felix and Drusilla, his Jewish wife (24:24-27). She was the youngest daughter of Herod Agrippa I, whose death was described earlier (12:20-23). Also, she was the sister of Agrippa II and Bernice, before whom Paul would testify later (25:13—26:32). She had abandoned her husband Azizus, King of Emesa, to become the third wife of Felix.

When summoned, Paul spoke to Felix and Drusilla about faith in Christ Jesus, emphasizing the themes of righteousness, self-control, and future judgment (24:24-25). To be sure, these were not welcome subjects for hearers who did not adhere to marital vows and had an itchy palm for bribes. Thus, Felix became alarmed, and dismissed Paul, saying that he would hear him at a later time. Luke recorded that he did converse with Paul quite often, but apparently remained more interested in bribes than the gospel (24:26).

Two years elapsed from the beginning of Paul's imprisonment in Caesarea until Felix was recalled to Rome to answer Jewish complaints against his misrule. Eager to ingratiate himself with the offended Jews as he left office, he left Paul in prison.

A few scholars believe that Paul wrote the Prison Letters (Ephesians, Philippians, Colossians, and Philemon) from Caesarea rather than Rome.

Appeal to Caesar (25:1-12; Focal: 25:1-12)

Festus succeeded Felix as the Roman governor of Judea, and shortly after his arrival in Caesarea, he went up to Jerusalem (v. 1). Though two years or more had elapsed since Paul's alleged desecration of the temple, Jewish feelings against him continued unabated. Thus with the change in provincial leaders, they sought again to destroy him. This time they hoped to persuade Festus to return Paul to Jerusalem to stand trial. All the while, they were plotting an ambush to kill him on the way (vv. 2-3). However, Festus affirmed that Paul was being kept in custody at Caesarea. He himself planned to return there soon, and he invited the Jewish leaders to press their charges against Paul in the provincial court (vv. 4-5).

Eight or ten days later Festus returned to Caesarea, accompanied by the Jewish leaders (v. 6). On the following day, he took his seat on the tribunal and ordered Paul to be brought before him. In the earlier trial before Felix, the lawyer Tertullus had specified the Jewish charges against Paul (24:5-6). However, Luke simply stated that the Jews brought many serious charges against him that they could not prove (v. 7). And Paul's defense was recorded in a single verse, "I have committed no offense either against the Law of the Jews or against the temple or against Caesar" (v. 8)

When Festus probed Paul's willingness to stand trial before him in Jerusalem, Paul refused (vv. 9-10). Perhaps he recalled the earlier plots against his life there, and doubted that he would survive to appear in court. At any rate, he felt that his case should be tried before Caesar's tribunal. Had he done anything that merited a capital sentence, he would not seek to avoid execution. However, he maintained his innocence, and to avoid being handed over to his own people, Paul exercised his right as a Roman citizen to appeal to Caesar (v. 11).

After a brief conference with his council, Festus responded, "You have appealed to Caesar, to Caesar you shall go" (v. 12).

Not Disobedient to the Heavenly Vision (26:19-29)

Evidently the appeal to Caesar was irrevocable, and the next step for Felix was to have Paul taken under custody to Rome. Yet he was perplexed about the legal brief he was expected to prepare to accompany the prisoner.

Several aspects of Paul's case remained obscure to him. Thus he sought help from King Agrippa II, son of Herod Agrippa I (12:1-23) and brother of Bernice and Drusilla (24:24). Both he and his sister Bernice had come to Caesarea to pay their respects to the new Roman governor of Judea (25:13). And Festus used the occasion of their visit to detail Paul's case for them and to draw on their greater knowledge of Jewish religious customs (25:14-21). When Agrippa II expressed an interest in the case, Festus promptly scheduled a hearing for the next day (25:22). Many government officials and prominent civic leaders gathered in the audience hall of the Praetorium for the occasion, and after a brief introduction by Festus, Paul was invited to speak (25:23-27).

Much of Paul's testimony in the great audience hall of Caesarea necessarily covered the same ground as his earlier testimony from the barracks stairs in Jerusalem (22:1-21). After a gracious introduction, Paul described his upbringing as a Jew and his later identification with the Pharisees (26:2-5). He reaffirmed his conviction that he was standing trial because of his belief in the resurrection of the dead (26:6-8). He reviewed his former role as a persecutor of Christians, mentioning again his mission to Damascus to arrest those who sought refuge there (26:9-12). Once more, he related his dramatic encounter with the risen Christ on his way into the city. As a result, Paul was converted and called to be an apostle to the Gentiles (26:13-18).

In obedience to this heavenly vision Paul preached the gospel in Damascus, Jerusalem and its environs, and even to the Gentiles (26:19-20). Everywhere he called on people to repent and turn to God and then to live out their faith. This was the real reason for the Jewish hostility toward him (26:21). Actually his message was thoroughly in keeping with "what the Prophets and Moses said was going to take place" (26:22). They had declared that the Christ was to fulfill His mission through suffering, death, and resurrection. By reason of His resurrection from the dead, He would "be the first to proclaim light both to the Jewish people and to the Gentiles" (26:23). Indeed, His message would become the gospel for all people.

At this point in Paul's defense, Festus exclaimed that Paul was out of his mind, robbed of reason by his great learning (26:24). Respectfully Paul maintained both his sanity and the truth of his utterance (26:25). Turning his attention again to Agrippa II, Paul expressed confidence in the king's knowledge of what he had stated about Jesus Christ (26:26). Then he said to the king boldly, "King Agrippa, do you believe the Prophets? I know that you do" (26:27). Some translations of verse 28 render the king's answer as though he were expressing a readiness to become a Christian (KJV; Phillips). However, I see the Greek text as saying that he was expressing both surprise and disdain regarding Paul's fervor, "Do you think that in such a short time you can persuade me to be a Christian?" (NIV)[2]

In Paul's reply to the king's annoyed reproof, Paul expressed the desire that all his hearers would share his faith (26:29). With these final words from Paul, the king, Festus, Bernice, and those sitting with them arose and drew aside to confer. All concurred that Paul had done nothing worthy of death or imprisonment (26:31). "And Agrippa said to Festus, 'This man might have been set free if he had not appealed to Caesar'" (26:32).

Lessons for Life from Acts 21:15—26:32

Defenders of truth cannot be distorters of truth.—Those who see themselves as the defenders of the faith sometimes resort to half truths, outright falsehoods, and violent oppression against those who deviate from their stated beliefs. This lamentable spirit was revealed in the Asian Jews who falsely charged Paul with taking a Gentile into a forbidden area of the temple. Mere supposition, rather than proof, underlaid the charge that placed Paul's life in jeopardy. One gets the feeling that these Asian Jews were seizing an opportunity in Jerusalem to settle a score on an old grievance in Ephesus.

Our close friends before we were converted will reveal varying responses to our Christian testimonies.—Those who have experienced Jesus Christ as Lord will rejoice with us, they will listen intently to our account of God's gracious dealings with us. Some will be impressed by the change that the Lord has brought into our lives and will be open to our witness. Others may become distant and drop us from their circle, and some may express scorn or hostility (see 1 Pet. 4:3-5).

The gospel of Jesus Christ results in ethical living.—As Paul spoke to Felix and Drusilla about faith in Jesus Christ, he emphasized righteousness, self-control, and the judgment to come. These themes were intrinsic to the gospel of salvation, and particularly appropriate for the Roman governor and his spouse. Eschatological hope places a creative ethical tension at the heart of Christian discipleship.

---

1. Notices in Greek and Latin were posted, warning that any foreigner who intruded into the forbidden areas of the temple would be put to death. F. F. Bruce, *Commentary on the Book of Acts* (Grand Rapids, MI: Wm. B. Eerdmans Pub. Co., 1973) 434, provides the translation of one of them, " 'No foreigner may enter within the barricade which surrounds the temple and enclosure. Anyone who is caught doing so will have himself to blame for his ensuing death.' "

2. From the Holy Bible, *New International Version*, copyright © 1973, 1978, 1984 by International Bible Society.

Personal Learning Activities

1. True _____ False _____ When church leaders in Jerusalem heard about Paul's ministry among the Gentiles, they glorified God and advised that he make a vow in the temple (21:17-25).

2. True _____ False _____ Paul took some Gentiles into the temple to prove that they could be saved without being Jewish proselytes (21:15-26).

3. True _____ False _____ Paul was rescued from an angry mob by Roman soldiers (21:27-36).

4. In addressing the enraged Jews, Paul spoke in the _____ dialect to quiet his hearers (22:2).

5. Give four points of Paul's defense (22:3-11).
   (1) _____ (2) _____
   (3) _____ (4) _____ .

6. Underline the correct answer. Because Paul was a Roman citizen, he was (1) released, (2) kept from being severely beaten, (3) assured a place in heaven (22:28-29).

7. What subject caused a debate among the Jews and lightened the pressure on Paul? _____ (23:6-7).

8. God promised Paul: "Take _____; for as you have solemnly witnessed to My cause at _____, so you must witness at _____ also" (23:11).

9. Because of a threat on Paul's life, the commander had Paul transferred to _____ (23:23-24).

10. Paul remained in prison in Caesarea at least _____ years (24:27).
11. What three subjects did Paul stress when speaking to Felix and Drusilla (24:24-25)? (1) _____ (2) _____ (3) _____ _____ _____ _____ .
12. When Paul was brought for trial before Festus, he declared: "I have committed no offense either against _____ _____ _____ _____ or against the _____ or against _____ (25:8).
13. True _____ False _____ Festus refused to allow Paul to be sent to Rome for trial before Caesar even though he knew Paul was a Roman citizen (25:11-12; 26:32).
14. True _____ False _____ In his defense before Agrippa Paul told how he met Jesus and how he knew that Jesus was the Christ (26:1-23).
15. Write out a description of how you met Jesus _____ _____ _____ .

9

The Gospel for the Whole World

Acts 27:1—28:31

Much has happened since Luke recorded the risen Lord's command for His disciples to evangelize the world (1:8). There they were promised the Holy Spirit's power that would equip them to become His witnesses in Jerusalem, Judea, Samaria, and to the remotest part of the earth.

In the chapters that followed, Luke recorded much about the expansion of the gospel over the ancient Mediterranean world. Through Peter's sermon at Pentecost, religious pilgrims from distant lands heard the gospel. Then many returned home with it (2:5-42). Through the persecution that followed Stephen's martyrdom, the gospel spread throughout Judea and Samaria (8:4-25). And during a time of fasting and praying in the church at Antioch, the Gentile mission was born (13:1-3). Paul and his companions' three missionary journeys were a direct consequence of this meeting (13:1—14:28; 15:36—18:22; 18:23—21:16).

The gospel expansion was not geographical only, for there were cultural barriers to overcome also. The Jewish religious establishment was hostile toward apostolic preaching, and resorted to threats, beatings, and imprisonment to silence it (4:1—5:42). Ancient prejudices had to be overcome in the Jewish Christian evangelization of Samaria (8:4-25). Also, as a Jew, Peter stumbled at the threshold of the home of Cornelius, a God-fearing Gentile (10:28). Even within the ranks of Jewish believers, some were inclined to demand circumcision in addition to faith in Jesus Christ as a requirement for salvation (15:1-35). And in the Philippian jailer's conversion, the gospel had to overcome the barriers of paganism.

With this review of the geographical and cultural triumphs of the gospel before us, we move into the study of Acts 27:1— 28:31. Luke recorded Paul's voyage to Rome as a prisoner. In the provincial court of Festus, he had made his appeal to Caesar (25:9-12), and the time had come for him to be taken to Rome. With great skill, Luke described the dramatic events of Paul's voyage (27:1—28:15). He added a brief account of Paul's arrival in Rome and his subsequent ministry while awaiting trial in the imperial court (28:16-31). As always since his conversion, whether in or out of prison, Paul continued to bear testimony for the Lord Jesus Christ to all who came near him.

A Storm at Sea (27:21-25)

In the final "we" passage of Acts (27:1—28:16), Luke recorded Paul's voyage under custody to Rome. Along with other prisoners, he was placed under the command of "a centurion of the Augustan cohort named Julius" (v. 1). Aristarchus, who was a Macedonian of Thessalonica (20:4), and presumably Luke accompanied Paul (v. 2). The first port of call was Sidon, a Phoenician city located about 70 miles north of Caesarea. There a kindly Julius permitted Paul to visit fellow-Christians, who ministered to him (v. 3). Putting out to sea from Sidon, they sailed along the coast of Cilicia and Pamphylia until they came to Myra in Lycia (vv. 4-5).

Myra was an important port for a fleet of ships that transported grain from Egypt to Rome. In fact, many of these large grain ships were employed by the Roman government. When the centurion found one that was sailing for Italy, he put the prisoners in his charge aboard it (v. 6).

Progress was slow as the ship sailed from Myra in the direction of Cnidus, because a strong northwest wind was blowing (v. 7). Thus the captain determined to make a run for Crete, eventually docking in Fair Havens, a port near the city of Lasea (v. 8).

The voyage to this point had taken considerable time, and the season had come in which it was dangerous to set sail on the Mediterranean. Luke indicated that the Day of Atonement already had passed, marking a time in late September or early

October (v. 9). Mid-September was regarded as the end of the season for safe navigation in these waters, and after mid-November regular voyages ceased because of winter storms.

As an experienced traveler, Paul was in a position to counsel against continuing the voyage at that particular time (v. 10). After all, he had been shipwrecked on three previous occasions, and had spent a night and a day in the deep (2 Cor. 11:25). But the centurion yielded to the persuasion of the pilot and the captain of the ship to try to reach Phoenix, a Cretan harbor deemed more suitable for wintering (vv. 11-12). Thus when a favorable south wind came up, they weighed anchor and headed for Phoenix, sailing close to the shore (v. 13)

Then suddenly a violent wind called Euraquilo rushed down from the land and whipped the sea into a fury (v. 14). **Euraquilo** is a compound word that means, *northeaster,* so named by sailors who dreaded its awesome force.

Unable to face the ship into the wind, they had no choice but to give way to it (v. 15). Driven under the shelter of Clauda, a small island, they managed to hoist up the dinghy in tow and to undergird the ship with supporting cables (vv. 10-17). To avoid running aground on the Greater Syrtis, the dreaded quicksands off the African coast to the west of Cyrene, they let down a sea anchor. The following day they began to jettison cargo, and on the third day the spare gear was thrown overboard (vv. 18-19). Unable to see either sun or stars while the tempest raged for several days, the hope of survival was gradually abandoned (v. 20).

Then in the midst of the storm, Paul began to speak. He was unable to refrain from chiding those who at Fair Havens had ignored his warning against putting out to sea (v. 21). However, he had more than a rebuke to deliver. He described a vision in which an angel of God had appeared to him the previous night with the assurance that there would be no loss of life among them (v. 22). To be sure, the ship would run aground on a certain island and be lost (v. 26), but the lives of all aboard would be spared. God intended that Paul stand before Caesar in Rome, and His providential care would bring it to pass (v. 24). Thus, reassured by a divine visitation, Paul was able to urge his despairing shipmates to keep up their courage (v. 25).

Shipwrecked off Malta (27:39-44)

On the fourteenth night of the storm, the sailors began to sense that they were approaching land (v. 27). This was confirmed by two soundings, the second of which revealed a lesser depth than the first (v. 28). They also may have been able to hear the sound of breakers on a beach obscured by the darkness. Faced with the danger of running aground on rocks, they dropped four anchors from the stern and anxiously awaited daybreak (v. 29).

At this point, Luke described the sailors' plot to escape from the ship in the dinghy. Under the pretense of laying out anchors from the bow, they had lowered it into the sea (v. 30). But Paul warned the centurion and soldiers about the plan (v. 31). Whereupon the soldiers cut away the ropes that held the dinghy to the ship, and let it drift away (v. 32). This appeared to be a rash act, for it deprived the ship of the means of transporting the passengers in relays to the shore.

As the day was about to dawn, Paul encouraged all aboard to take some food. For many days they had eaten little or nothing, and were weakened. They needed the nourishment that would replenish their strength (v. 34). Having reassured them again that no lives would be lost, Paul took bread, thanked God in the presence of all, broke it, and began to eat (v. 35). Paul's example and words encouraged the others, and they also ate (v. 36). Here Luke recorded that 276 persons were aboard the ship (v. 37). Perhaps the numbering of the passengers was related to the apportioning of the food. Then after all had eaten, they lightened the ship by throwing the rest of the wheat into the sea. This was done so that the ship would draw as little water as possible as it drifted toward the shore.

Day finally came, but none aboard was able to recognize the bay before them. Their plan was to drive the ship onto the beach. To this end, they cast off the four anchors which had been let out from the stern, leaving them in the sea. They loosened the ropes of the large steering paddles, one on each side of the ship, that functioned as rudders. And they hoisted the foresail to the wind, as they prepared to run the ship aground on the beach (v. 40).

But then, at a place "where two seas met," they struck a reef (v. 41). The prow of the vessel stuck fast in the sand and mud, while the stern began to break up under the relentless assault of the waves. Since the soldiers' lives would be forfeited if the prisoners in their custody escaped, they planned to kill them (v. 42). However, the centurion, who had had much reason throughout the hazardous voyage to appreciate Paul, intervened and denied their intention. Rather, he commanded all who could swim to jump overboard first and head for the shore (v. 43). Then the rest could follow, holding onto planks or other parts of the wreckage, until all reached land safely (v. 44).

Ministry on Malta (28:1-11)

Once ashore, they learned that they had landed on the island of Malta, some 60 miles south of the nearest tip of Sicily (28:1). Many of the island's inhabitants had lined the beach to witness the dramatic shipwreck and rescue operation. Moreover, since it was a cold, rainy October morning, they had built a fire to warm the chilled and drenched survivors (28:2). Not content to warm himself at the fire while others sought wood to sustain it, Paul also gathered a bundle of sticks and laid it on the fire. As he did so, a snake, unnoticed in the bundle he had gathered, came out because of the heat and bit him on the hand (28:3).

When the natives saw the snake hanging from Paul's hand, they had a ready explanation: *he was a murderer!* He should have received the punishment he deserved by drowning at sea; yet, he had survived. However, "justice" had not tolerated his escape, and through a scorched serpent had carried out a back-up plan to kill him. While Paul shook the snake off his hand into the flames, they looked on, fully expecting him to bloat up or suddenly keel over. But neither happened. Thus they soon revised their shoreline theology and concluded: *he was a god!* (See also 14:11-13.)

From murderer to deity in moments, because of a snake bite. What a change!

Paul was not wrapping the snake around his neck or fondling it as a demonstration to the Maltese of his faith in God. Rather while doing a sensible thing—gathering fire wood—he was bitten by a snake. The mishap was consequential, not a demonstration or a performance.

To distinguish *faith in God* from *presumption on God* is necessary! Presumption on God usually masquerades as super-faith, and the superficial accept it as such. Actually, it is an expression of insidious doubt that repeatedly concocts bizarre crises in an effort to force God to prove He is on the premises.

Due to the winter season, the survivors of the shipwreck remained on Malta for the next three months (November through January). During this time, Paul continued his ministry. He healed the father of Publius, "the leading man of the island" (28:7-8). He healed others also, and in turn was treated with honor and generous provisions (28:9-10).

Travel to Rome (28:12-15)

But at the end of the winter season, they put out to sea again and eventually reached Puteoli, the principal port of southern Italy (28:11-13). It was also the main terminal for the fleet of Alexandrian grain ships.

After a stopover of seven days in Puteoli, the travelers continued on their way to Rome (28:14). Paul was encouraged greatly, when Roman Christians came out to meet him at the Market of Appius, about 40 miles from the city. Ten miles further along at the Three Inns, a second deputation of Roman believers joined him (28:15). Thus Paul was well attended, as he made his way to stand trial in the imperial city.

Under Custody in Rome (28:16-31)

Preliminary Meeting with the Jewish Leaders (vv. 16-22)

When Paul arrived in Rome, he was permitted to stay in his own rented quarters, guarded by a soldier (v. 16). After three days, he called a meeting of the Jewish leaders in an effort to secure their understanding of his circumstances. He explained that he had done nothing against his people or their ancestral traditions; yet, he had been delivered from Jerusalem into the hands of the Romans (v. 17). After examining him, the Romans were willing to release him, having found no ground for putting him to death (v. 18). Yet the Jews objected, forcing him to appeal to Caesar, though he had no accusation against his own people (v. 19). For this reason, Paul had requested an audience with the Jewish religious leaders in Rome. He wanted them to know that he was a prisoner "for the sake of the hope of Israel" (v. 20). For he believed that the Christian gospel he proclaimed was the true fulfillment of Israel's messianic hope (see 26:6-7).

In response to Paul's plea, the Jewish leaders denied that they had received any letters from Judea about him. They had not heard anything bad about him from any who had come to Rome (v. 21). Then they expressed a desire to hear Paul's views, acknowledging that the "sect" he represented was widely known and badly reputed everywhere (v. 22).

How were the Jewish leaders in Rome able to disclaim any firsthand knowledge of Christianity? Though Christian origins in the city have remained an unresolved problem, we have reasons for believing that the church was well established by the time of Paul's arrival. Jewish visitors from Rome had been present in Jerusalem on the day of Pentecost (2:10). Again, the disturbances in the Jewish quarters that led Claudius to banish Jews from Rome likely were caused by a vigorous preaching of the gospel (18:2). Furthermore, at the time that Paul wrote his letter to the Romans, the church already had attained a widespread reputation for faithfulness (Rom. 1:8). And had not two groups of Roman Christians met Paul on his way to the city (28:15)? Thus it remains difficult to believe that the Jewish religious leaders in Rome had only a hearsay knowledge of Christianity. They may have had their own reasons for not revealing all they knew.

Second Meeting with the Jews (vv. 23-29)

On the day set for the meeting with the Jews, a large number gathered at Paul's lodging. From morning to night, he solemnly testified to them about the kingdom of God. As was his custom in witnessing to his fellow Jews, Paul sought to prove from both the Law of Moses and the Prophets that Jesus was the Christ (v. 23; 13:17-41; 17:2-3,10-11; 26:22-23). However, at the end of a long day, the response of his Jewish hearers was divided. Some believed, but apparently the greater number disbelieved and turned away (v. 24). Then Paul admonished them with God's words to Isaiah the prophet (vv. 26-27; Isa. 6:9-10). Though God had sent Isaiah to the people, he was warned that they would not heed his message. Jesus cited this same passage to describe the Jews' rejection of Him (Matt. 13:14-15; Mark 4:12; Luke 8:10; John 12:39-40). And now the prophetic words equally applied to the Jews of Rome. Henceforth, the gospel would be proclaimed primarily to the Gentiles, and they would listen (v. 28). Verse 29 is not found in the earliest and best texts. Thus it is a bracketed reading in the *New American Standard Bible.*

Openly Preaching the Kingdom of God (vv. 30-31)

To end his account of Christianity's triumphant spread in its earliest decades, Luke used two verses to summarize Paul's two-year ministry in Rome. Bound by a wrist-chain to a Roman soldier, Paul was not free to move about the city, as he had earlier in Philippi, Corinth, or Ephesus. However, the Roman authorities permitted him to welcome all who came to him (v. 30). Furthermore, they placed no restrictions on his message. He was free to preach the kingdom of God and to teach concerning the Lord Jesus Christ. He did both openly and without hindrance in the capital city of the Roman Empire. That Paul proclaimed the gospel that could not be bound was of great significance. Indeed, this has been affirmed and repeated under all sorts of circumstances from the beginning of the Book of Acts. During Paul's ministry as a prisoner in Rome the gospel still could not be bound. Those who were free to hear Paul expound the marvelous message of God's kingdom also were free to take it back to their homes and communities. Furthermore, prisoners often were permitted to send letters to places where they were unable to go. Paul did this. A solid tradition indicates that Paul wrote the Prison Letters (Eph., Phil., Col., and Philem.) during his confinement in Rome. And what about the soldiers assigned the duty of guarding Paul? Could more than one of them have prayed to receive Jesus Christ as Lord and Savior while chained to his wrist (Phil. 1:12-13)?

Some scholars have felt that the Book of Acts ends abruptly, leaving the reader with a feeling of suspense. Luke gave a detailed account of Paul's trials before the Jewish council and the Roman provincial court, but he did not tell the outcome of his trial in Rome. Devout scholars have proposed a wide range of explanations: (1) Acts ends as it does, because Luke already had described what had happened up to the time of writing. (2) Luke intended to write a third book as a sequel to Luke-Acts. (3) Something happened to Luke to keep him from continuing his account. (4) To have recorded Paul's execution would have limited or embarrassed the value of Acts as a Christian defense.

But others have insisted that Luke never intended to write Paul's biography. Rather, he purposed to describe the gospel's expansion from the Jewish religious capital of Jerusalem to the world city of Rome. In doing so, he recorded the gospel's triumph over many cultural barriers that stood in the way of its progress. In the Book of Acts, Luke admirably achieved his purpose of presenting the gospel of Jesus Christ as the gospel for all people.

Lessons for Life from Acts 27:1—28:31

Our lives as Christians may be affected greatly by the quality of decisions that others make.—This is particularly true of those who exercise authority over us. Imagine a Julius having the power to make a decision that would endanger a Paul's life, as well as all others aboard ship. Paul was not at liberty to say, "If you want to risk your lives in a winter storm at sea, that is your prerogative, but I'm staying in Fair Havens until it's safe to navigate." He was not a tourist on a Mediterranean cruise; rather he was a prisoner under the command of a Roman officer.

The great promise of Romans 8:28-29, written shortly before Paul left Greece on his final trip to Jerusalem, has to work out in a world that includes persecution and shipwreck.

We are stewards of all that happens to us, tragedies as well as triumphs.—On a ship at sea, battered by a storm for almost two weeks, Paul was able to hear God's voice and to share His message of hope. Through his stewardship of faith and circumstances God was able to encourage the despairing passengers. Today, some people we seek to win to Jesus Christ may be influenced more by our stewardship of adversity than by any words spoken in fair weather.

Faith in God honors Him, whereas presumption on God dishonors Him and degrades us.—Jesus called a suggested leap from the Temple an act that would make trial of God (Matt. 4:5-7; Luke 4:9-13).

Faith waits patiently for the Lord to lead whereas presumption acts rashly and imagines that God has nothing better to do than pull the consequences out of our folly.

Faith responds; presumption manipulates!

The Book of Acts, above all else, is a book of Holy Spirit-inspired witnessing.—Acts is a witness to God's saving grace through faith in Jesus Christ, intended for all. This was true at Pentecost when Luke began his record. Likewise, it was true when Acts ended, for Paul, a prisoner, was bearing a faithful witness for Jesus Christ to all who came to him. Ever since, the same Holy Spirit has been writing Acts 29 through the witnessing of all who are committed to Jesus Christ as Lord.

Personal Learning Activities

1. Evidence (the word "we") shows that Paul's physician friend, _____, accompanied him on his voyage to Rome

(27:1-2).

2. Underline the correct answer. On the journey to Rome, Paul was treated (1) with abusive disrespect, (2) with respect and a certain freedom.

3. True _____ False _____ Because Paul was both a seasoned traveler and a Christian, the captain of the ship heeded his advice and delayed sailing (27:10-13).

4. True _____ False _____ When caught in a great storm at sea, the captain ordered the crew to get rid of all excess cargo and equipment and thus saved the ship (27:18-44).

5. Based on a message from _____, Paul stated that even though the ship would be lost, everyone would be saved and advised all to _____ (27:20-25).

6. True _____ False _____ The centurion's respect for Paul led him to keep the soldiers from killing all the prisoners and to allow all to try to get to shore (27:42-44).

7. When a snake bit Paul, the residents of the island of Malta thought he was a _____ but when he was unaffected, they decided he was a _____ (28:1-6).

8. Luke said little about Paul's ministry on Malta, but indicated that God used him to _____ _____ _____ (28:7-9).

9. Paul was encouraged on the final portion of his journey to Rome by _____ _____ _____ _____ (28:14-15).

10. True _____ False _____ In Rome, Paul experienced freedom to communicate the gospel and began by sharing "the hope of Israel" with Jewish leaders of the city (28:16-22).

11. The response of the Jews to Paul's efforts to convince them that Jesus was the Messiah reveals the typical response in that some _____ and some _____ (28:23-24).

12. Luke summarized Paul's two years of ministry in Rome as "_____ the kingdom of God and _____ concerning the _____ Jesus _____ with all openness, unhindered" (28:31).

13. What commitment will you make in light of this study? _

_____

_____ .

How to Become a Christian

JESUS

Jesus Christ was with God the Father before the world was created. He became human and lived among humanity as Jesus of Nazareth. He came to reveal the Father. He lived, He ministered, He died upon a cross (John 1:1-18).

Jesus is the source of eternal life. He is available to people today because God has raised Jesus from the dead.

Jesus wants to be the doorway to new life for you. In the Bible He was called the "Lamb of God" (John 1:29). In the Old Testament a lamb was killed as a sacrifice for the sins of the people. Jesus became the sacrificial lamb for you.

Jesus said, "I am the way, the truth, and the life: no man cometh unto the Father, but by me" (John 14:6). He is waiting for you now. Here is what you must do to accept Him and become a Christian:

- Recognize His love for you. He died for you.
- Admit your need for Him. Confess your need for salvation.
- Express sorrow for your sin by repenting, which means turning away from sin and turning to God.
- Place your faith in Jesus and invite Him into your life.
- Pray a prayer of repentance and faith. If you do not know what to say to God, say something like, "Dear Heavenly Father, I know that you love me. I confess my sin and ask for your forgiveness. I now invite Jesus into my life. In Jesus' name. Amen."

Jesus is now your personal Savior. Tell a pastor or another Christian about your decision. Show others your faith in Christ by being baptized and becoming an active member of a church.

The Church Study Course

The Church Study Course is a Southern Baptist educational system consisting of short courses for adults and youth combined with a credit and recognition system. More than 500 courses are available in 23 subject areas. Credit is awarded for each course completed. These credits may be applied to one or more of the 100 plus diploma plans in the recognition system. Diplomas are available for most leadership positions as well as general diplomas for all Christians. These diplomas are the certification that a person has completed from five to eight prescribed courses. Diploma requirements are given in the catalogs.

Complete details about the Church Study Course system, courses available, and diplomas offered may be found in a current copy of the *Church Study Course Catalog*. Study course materials are available from Baptist Book Stores.

The Church Study Course system is sponsored by the Sunday School Board, Woman's Missionary Union, and Brotherhood Commission of the Southern Baptist Convention.

How to Request Credit for this Course

This book is the text for course number 04-121 in the subject area: "BIBLE STUDIES." This course is designed for five hours of group study.

Credit for this course may be obtained in two ways:

1. Read the book and attend class sessions. (If you are absent from one or more sessions, complete the "Personal Learning Activities for the material missed.)
2. Read the Book and complete the "Personal Learning Activities." (Written work should be submitted to an appropriate church leader.)

A request for credit may be made on Form 725 "Church Study Course Enrollment/Credit Request" and sent to the Awards Office, Sunday School Board, 127 Ninth Avenue, North, Nashville, Tennessee 37234. The form below may be used to request credit.

A record of your awards will be maintained by the Awards Office. Twice each year copies will be sent to churches for distribution to members.

CHURCH STUDY COURSE
ENROLLMENT/CREDIT REQUEST
FORM - 725 (Rev. 1-89)

MAIL THIS ➡ REQUEST TO

CHURCH STUDY COURSE AWARDS OFFICE
BAPTIST SUNDAY SCHOOL BOARD
127 NINTH AVENUE, NORTH
NASHVILLE, TENNESSEE 37234

Is this the first course taken since 1983? ☐ YES If yes, or not sure complete all of Section 1. ☐ NO If no, complete only bold boxes in Section 1.

SECTION 1 - STUDENT INFO.

STUDENT

☐ Mr.
☐ Mrs.
☐ Miss

Name (First, MI, Last)

Street, Route, or P.O. Box

City, State   Zip Code

Personal CSC Number* ⬇

DATE OF BIRTH
Month | Day | Year

Social Security Number

CHURCH

Church Name

Mailing Address

City, State   Zip Code

SECTION 2 - CHANGE REQUEST ONLY (Current inf. in Section1)

☐ Former Name

☐ Former Address   Zip Code

☐ Former Church   Zip Code

SECTION 3 - COURSE CREDIT REQUEST

Course No.	Title (use exact title)
1. 04-121	**Acts: The Gospel for All People.**
2.	
3.	
4.	
5.	
6.	

SECTION 4 - DIPLOMA ENROLLMENT

Enter exact diploma title from current Church Study Course catalog. Indicate diploma age group if appropriate. Do not enroll again with each course. When all requirements have been met, the diploma will be mailed to your church. Enrollment in Christian Development Diplomas is automatic. No charge will be made for enrollment or diplomas.

Title of Diploma	Age group or area
Title of Diploma	Age group or area

Signature of Pastor, Teacher, or Other Church Leader | Date

*CSC # not required for new students. Others please give CSC # when using SS # for the first time. Then, only one ID # is required.